GROUP COMMUNICATION

Cases for Analysis, Appreciation and Application

Edited by
Laura W. Black

Kendall Hunt
publishing company

Cover images © Shutterstock, Inc.

www.kendallhunt.com
Send all inquiries to:
4050 Westmark Drive
Dubuque, IA 52004-1840

Copyright © 2010 by Kendall Hunt Publishing Company

ISBN 978-0-7575-8295-0

Printed in the United States of America
10   9   8   7   6   5   4   3   2

CONTENTS

Group Development, Roles, and Norms 35

Group Climate and Relational Communication 63

Conflict in Groups **91**

Problem Solving and Decision Making............. 125

Groups and Democracy 157

PREFACE FOR INSTRUCTORS

Laura W. Black, Abbey E. Wojno, and Courtney E. Cole

As the vast literature on group communication demonstrates, group interaction is pervasive in human life. People participate in groups in families, in schools, at work, online, in community organizations, and in sports and recreation. This book highlights the pervasiveness of group life by providing narrative cases of groups in a wide range of contexts. As Naumes and Naumes (1999) remind us, using case studies in the classroom provides students with the opportunity to actively participate in the process of learning and see theory play out in actual occurrences. Cases that highlight group life are important pedagogical tools because they encourage students to discuss, analyze, and develop a grounded understanding of group communication theory and practices.

This book is filled with stories of real groups in real contexts. Such groups include hospital teams, a Nicaraguan coffee cooperative, a kayaking trip, civic leaders holding a citizen discussion, a student senate, online groups, a community choir, grocery co-op employees, a basketball team, a school board, a dance troupe, and a jury. Written as narratives, our cases draw from the original research and/or lived experience of well-known and up-and-coming group communication scholars. The stories are realistic, vivid, engaging, and provide compelling examples of group interaction with lively dialogue and an insider's view of group life. As such, our cases can bring group communication concepts/theory to life and help students empathize with characters who encounter challenges and successes in group life.

ANALYSIS, APPRECIATION, AND APPLICATION

A distinguishing feature of this casebook is that it highlights two different approaches to understanding group interaction. The first is *critical analysis*. Many of the cases center on a dilemma, challenge, or problem faced by the group or one of its members. Such cases end with the events unresolved to provide readers with the opportunity to consider alternative solutions. The goal of these cases is to encourage readers to discuss, analyze, and develop criteria as well as potential solutions to the problems illustrated in the case (Naumes and Naumes 1999).

Alternately, and unique in comparison to most casebooks, other cases in this text highlight examples of successful group communication practices. Rather than centering on the problems faced by the group, these cases demonstrate the process and outcomes of highly successful group interactions. These cases may still highlight challenging interactions, but they prominently feature descriptions of how problems were resolved or productively dealt with through the group's interaction. The goal of these cases is to engage learners in a kind of *appreciative inquiry* about the success of effective group practices and to consider the extent to which particular communication theory and practices can be applied to other groups and contexts.

Appreciative inquiry has gained the attention of some prominent communication scholars (see Barge et al. 2008; Dura and Singhal 2009; Singhal, Sternin, and Dura 2009). Learning from an appreciative standpoint, in contrast to a critical approach, encourages learners to begin with the recognition that something within the group is working well (Barrett 1995). Students are then invited to "discover, describe, and explain those exceptional moments in which systems function well" (Barrett 1995, 39). As students participate in these "generative conversations" discussions should shift from focusing on "what is" to envisioning potentialities of small group interactions (Barrett 1995). Rather than focusing purely on problem solving, analyzing groups through an appreciative standpoint provides students with the opportunity to "accentuate successes of the past, evoke images of possible futures, and create a spirit of restless ongoing inquiry" (Barrett 1995, 40). Several cases in this book are designed to help students engage in this kind of appreciative process.

ORGANIZATION OF THE BOOK

The book is organized into sections that mirror the organization of many small group communication textbooks. Yet, because the cases are realistic depictions of group life, each case can be used to explore a variety of group communication concepts, even those ranging beyond the category to which the case is assigned. For this reason, the table of contents provides a brief description of each case and a list of keywords that highlight the major concepts illustrated in the case.

We made a conscious choice not to create a separate section on diversity in small groups. Rather, diversity is a value that has been infused throughout this book. It has been carefully edited to include a broad spectrum of cases that represent different types of small groups and a diverse range of group members. There are cases that address online groups, groups in educational contexts, recreational, civic, and community groups, as well as groups in nonprofit and for-profit settings. Within cases, there are characters of different ages, ethnicities and nationalities, education, and experiences. The cases in this book highlight both significant challenges and successes in regard to diversity and allow students to consider how diversity interfaces with other aspects of group life. Similarly, aspects of ethics are woven throughout the cases and evident in all the major sections of the book.

The first major section of the book deals with *group characteristics*. The cases in this section focus primarily on how groups are defined, how they are organized, and how they are connected to the larger contexts in which they exist. These cases offer the opportunity to discuss group members' interdependence, group structure, group identity, and the environments in which groups function.

The second section of the book deals with *group development, roles, and norms*. In this section, the cases deal with how group develop and change over time, the implicit and explicit behavioral expectations that characterize different groups, and the different sorts of positions implicit in groups. These cases allow readers to consider issues of group development, the emergence and enforcement of group norms, and group member roles, including leadership.

The third section of the book focuses on *group climate and relational communication* in groups. These cases deal with the emotional environment and relationship-building in groups and highlight issues of task and relational communication. Some of these cases illustrate how social support happens in computer-mediated groups; another looks at the benefits and detriments of a competitive climate for a varsity basketball team.

The fourth section of the book engages issues of *conflict within groups*. These cases provide examples of how conflict begins, escalates, and can be managed in groups. In the fifth section, the book features cases on *problem solving and decision making*. The cases in this section consider two of the pervasive tasks faced by groups. Some cases highlight common decision-making struggles, while others provide examples of groups successfully dealing with difficult choices. These cases highlight ethical challenges faced by groups when making difficult decisions or addressing real, complex problems.

The final section of the book highlights the role of small *groups in democracy*. Cases in this section highlight the connection between group discussion and larger democratic systems in which groups are embedded. One of these cases highlights the consensus decision processes in an employee-run grocery co-op. Another case highlights how parliamentary procedure enables and constrains deliberative discussion in a student senate. The final cases in this section demonstrate how the structure of a community and group facilitation processes can allow for successful public deliberation and civic engagement for community groups. This section provides an opportunity to discuss how groups are a part of civic life, and also provides examples of meeting management, facilitation, leadership, and decision making.

ONLINE TEACHING RESOURCES

Pedagogical materials accompany each case, which may be accessed through our publisher's website at http://www.kendallhunt.com. Inspired by Lynn's (1999) discussion of teaching notes, these materials include short abstracts summarizing each case narrative and detailed teaching/learning objectives that address the purposes and goals of each case. The authors also offer lesson plans that outline possible discussions about the cases including proposed time allocation and approaches for opening and summing up the conversation. The pedagogical materials also include eight to ten discussion questions that instructors can use to aid students' analysis and appreciation of the events in the case. Finally, making these materials available online provides us the opportunity to include links to websites, photos, and videos that provide more information and insight about many of the groups highlighted throughout the book. It is our hope that all of these materials will be of value both to instructors as they plan their approach to incorporating cases into the classroom and to students as they analyze cases and make connections to theories and concepts addressed in their course.

A WORD OF THANKS

As editors, we have worked very closely with the authors whose work is represented in this book and we thank them for their efforts. We also have benefited greatly from the supportive and inspiring conversations with John Gastil, Joann Keyton, Lynn Harter, and Kevin Barge. John and Joann provided early feedback to some of the newer scholars whose work is represented in this book. Kevin, Joann, and Lynn helped us develop a better understanding of appreciative inquiry in relation to cases, and John's continued mentorship and friendship has been invaluable in making this book possible. We are grateful for their guidance and support.

WORKS CITED

Barge, J. K., M. Lee, K. Maddux, R. Nabring, and B. Townsend. 2008. Managing dualities in planned change initiatives. *Journal of Applied Communication Research* 36:364–390.

Barrett, F. J. 1995. Creating appreciative learning cultures. *Organizational Dynamics* 24:36–49.

Dura, L., and A. Singhal. 2009. *Will Ramon finish sixth grade? Positive deviance for student retention in rural Argentina.* Positive Deviance Wisdom Series 2, 1–8. Boston: Tufts University, Positive Deviance Initiative.

Lynn, Jr., L. E. 1999. *Teaching and learning with cases: A guidebook.* Chappaqua, NY: Seven Bridges Press.

Naumes, W., and Naumes, M. J. 1999. *The art and craft of case writing.* Thousand Oaks, CA: Sage.

Singhal, A., J. Sternin, and L. Dura. 2009. *Combating malnutrition in the land of a thousand rice fields: Positive deviance grows roots in Vietnam.* Positive Deviance Wisdom Series 1, 1–8. Boston: Tufts University, Positive Deviance Initiative.

STUDENT INTRODUCTION: HOW TO USE THIS BOOK

This book provides an important opportunity for you to enhance and apply your understanding of small group communication. The case studies in this book complement your small group communication textbook because they provide examples of real groups, in a wide range of contexts, dealing with the challenges and opportunities inherent in group life. Some cases are directly relevant to your current situation as college students; others focus on group communication in situations you are likely to encounter in the future.

All the cases in this book are based on experiences of real groups. This means that the cases are as complex as life itself. So, while cases have been grouped into sections, you will find that all the cases engage a number of group communication issues and concepts. Some of the cases demonstrate dilemmas, challenges, or problems faced by the group or its members and end without a clear resolution of the events in the case. The goal of these cases is to encourage you to discuss, analyze, and develop criteria as well as potential solutions to the problems illustrated in the case. Alternately, some cases highlight examples of successful group communication practices. Rather than solely describing problems faced by the group, these cases demonstrate how groups can be effective and ethical even when facing challenging circumstances. In these cases, it is important to consider what practices helped the groups be effective and how well these practices could be applied to other groups and contexts.

People reading the same case will often pay attention to different details and issues. Therefore, these cases provide an important starting point from which to discuss and delve into the complexities of group communication. As you read and think about cases in the book, consider the interactions and conversations between characters in the case. Try to imagine and understand the different characters' perspectives and consider what the group in the case could do to address their situation. There are discussion questions to help you think through these issues, but you also might find other ways to apply and test your knowledge of group communication concepts as you read these cases. In short, these cases offer the opportunity to use your knowledge of small group communication to analyze and consider how you might act in a variety of group contexts.

PART

Group Characteristics

COMMUNICATING FOR WELLNESS

Understanding the Dynamics of a School Health Advisory Team

Anne Gerbensky-Kerber

With limited time and resources, members of a school health team work to meet the needs of their community.

Stephanie Larson strode quickly down the long hallway connecting Sycamore Elementary and Junior High schools, dodging students who were opening their lockers to collect coats and books. "Bye, Mrs. Larson!" a few of them called to her before slamming their doors closed and scurrying toward the building's front entrance. Stephanie smiled and continued her brisk pace, pausing briefly to check her watch when she reached the door of the elementary school's teachers' lounge. It was nearly 3:15 p.m. "Looks like I'm right on schedule after all!" she thought as she opened the door. As the nurse for both schools, Stephanie had a number of end-of-the-day responsibilities, such as dispensing time-sensitive medications and checking a diabetic student's blood sugar levels. Today, she had rushed through these tasks in order to make it to the Sycamore schools' Health Advisory Committee's monthly meeting on time.

Once inside the room, she was greeted by Randy, the owner of a local farm, who also oversaw the junior high school's 4-H and agriculture clubs. Stephanie noticed immediately that his three young daughters were seated at one of the four round tables in the lounge with him. "I hope you don't mind that the girls are here with me today," he said. "My wife had to go out of town unexpectedly, and I wasn't able to find a babysitter on such short notice. It was either bring them with me or not come to the meeting at all."

Stephanie smiled. This wasn't the first time it had happened, but Randy's daughters, who ranged between four and eight years old, were typically very well behaved and quiet while the adults talked. "That's fine! I'm always glad that you're able to be here. I know how busy you and Julie are," she said, unloading copies of the meeting agenda and healthy snacks on a nearby table. Looking around, she commented, "I'm surprised that no one else is here yet."

"Oh, come on. You know we never get going on time!" Randy lightheartedly teased as he reached for a bag of unsalted almonds. "Seriously, we might think about revisiting the start time for these meetings. The teachers are always rushing to get here because of after-school activities. It might help us to recruit a few parents to help, too, since they would have time to get their children home and settled before the start of the meeting. Other than me, I don't even know who we have for parents on the committee anymore."

Stephanie mulled over his suggestion as she tore open the plastic surrounding a string cheese stick. "You know, we messed around with the meeting times about a couple of years ago. We played with lunch-hour meetings, then shifted it back to 4 p.m., and tried after-dinner hours, like 7:30 or 8 p.m. But all of our members also have work, families, and other commitments in the evenings. The 3:15 start time has worked the best for accommodating most people's schedules, even if the teachers have to come in late. But you're right. We need to get more parents involved. It might be time for us to revisit the issue, especially if you think timing is holding them back." As she sat down at one of the short plastic chairs at Randy's table, Stephanie glanced at her copy of the agenda. "It should be a relatively short meeting today. Be sure to bring that up when we get to 'Open Issues,' okay? I think it's a good thing for the group to talk about."

ASSEMBLING A SCHOOL HEALTH ADVISORY COMMITTEE

Stephanie sighed as she packed up papers after the meeting. Most of the group members had arrived late, and then needed to leave no later than 4:45 p.m. The discussion had focused primarily on logistics for an upcoming "Fun Run" event. "That's fine," she grumbled, "but a lot of what we talked about could have been dealt with by communicating outside of the meeting." The committee had not been able to talk about Randy's suggestion to adjust meeting times. Stephanie was also frustrated about how few participants had shown up. Granted, it was March and attendance typically dwindled as the school year went on. As she shut off the overhead lights in the lounge and closed the door behind her, she remembered how thankful she was for her regulars. "I can always count on Randy and Kelly from the County Health Department to be here." There were eager new faces to be hopeful about, too: Carolyn, the recently hired family-community partnership coordinator for the district, and Dan, a student teacher in physical education at the elementary school. But she could think of at least a half-dozen others who rarely attended meetings. "Maybe I should send an e-mail about being here or getting here on time," she thought as she walked through the halls back to her office. "Then again, they're all such busy, committed people. I should be grateful they're willing to help us out at all."

Pausing to admire a colorful mural outside a third-grade classroom, Stephanie pondered how the Health Advisory Committee had changed over time. In 2004, the school board had asked her to chair the group and recruit volunteers, including parents, teachers, school administrators and staff members, community partners and health providers, to participate. The group's first task had been to develop a district-wide health and wellness policy, a federal requirement for all school districts receiving funds for free, and reduced-price lunches. Since the group had already developed a policy, its focus over the last few years had shifted to planning health-related initiatives and events in the schools. As she continued walking, Stephanie lamented, "It's not like our work isn't good. We just could be doing so much more!" The Sycamore school district served students from three small towns in rural Appalachia that struggled with poverty, limited employment opportunities, and scarce health care resources. As a school nurse, she was particularly concerned about the increasing rates of childhood obesity and related health problems like diabetes. "Most of the families in our area can't afford healthy foods like fruits and vegetables. There aren't enough parks or playgrounds in our area, and kids can't even walk to school as a way to get exercise because the sidewalks are crumbling. This committee could be a place for working on solutions to these problems," she thought.

Finding committed community partners, like Kelly, had been easy. However, given the number of low-income families in the area, it had been difficult to find parents able to take time away from their job (or, in many cases, jobs) to join the group. Stephanie quickly found that the parents who did help were the ones who were already involved in other school activities. "And it's the same problem with the faculty and staff. The district can't afford to pay them to participate. There aren't many colleagues who will volunteer their time, and we just have to make do with what we get."

Though Stephanie had made the committee's meeting attendance policies flexible to accommodate members' schedules, she was beginning to get concerned that these policies were a little too flexible. "The quality of our work is really going to suffer if this goes much further," she thought as she unlocked and opened her office door. "And then, we'll be in serious trouble." Reaching for her coat and purse, Stephanie thought about the previous meeting when she had recruited volunteers to attend the annual Coordinated School Health Conference. The committee was obligated to send at least six representatives in order to maintain funding from a state-level grant. She hadn't been surprised that Randy, Kelly, and Carolyn volunteered to attend, but she was frustrated that she was still trying to secure at least two more people to go. "Don't people understand what is at stake here? We rely on these grants to fund our projects. It's not like there are unlimited places to get money, especially in this economy!"

Because the district was only twenty miles from a state university, the committee often hired interns and AmeriCorps volunteers from the education and nursing programs to help with specific projects. Kelly had also been willing to have her student workers assist as well. "While that's been terrific, they're always short-timers," Stephanie lamented, thinking of how many student workers had left after their funding ran out or they graduated. They just couldn't be relied upon for the group to produce a consistent effort, year after year. "We really need to talk about this in April," she resolved.

PLANNING THE NEWSLETTER

At the next meeting, Stephanie passed around copies of the agenda and encouraged people to help themselves to the apples and bottled water on the table. "I'm happy to welcome Jeff Miller, principal of Sycamore Junior High, to our meeting today," she said, gesturing to Jeff with a smile. While Stephanie was grateful Jeff attempted to participate in the committee meetings once or twice a year, her boss's presence made her feel a little more self-conscious than usual. Jeff nodded and said hello. The interns and volunteers went around the table introducing themselves, and Stephanie noted that the rest of the group already knew him.

"The first item on our agenda today is the summer newsletter," Stephanie announced. "I'm planning to distribute copies on June 1, which means that I need to collect articles from everyone no later than May 16. I'll send out an e-mail about this to teachers at the schools, too. I really want to make sure that we can stick with this due date. Last time, we received some great articles about a day or two before we went to print."

"Sorry about that," Dan said from across the table. "I'm guilty, too!" Carolyn responded. Stephanie smiled forgivingly at them. "That's okay! You weren't the only ones, either. I just want to make sure we don't repeat it, because it can be a hassle to reshuffle things. I think Amanda would appreciate not having to put in so many late-night hours this time."

Amanda, who was sitting at the opposite end of the table from Stephanie, nodded. "That would be great. It's not that we can't get it done, but I'm only allotted 15 hours per week for my internship here. It's helpful for me to be able to plan my schedule and any changes in advance."

Before she could finish, Jeff responded, "I think that's great, Stephanie. We really liked how the newsletter turned out last time, but I want to make sure we're doing a better job of getting stories from all of the schools. Most of the winter issue's articles focused on what was happening at the elementary school. It's important that we include more about the junior high and high schools, too. Maybe you should attend the next board of directors meeting and ask them to provide something as well."

Randy furrowed his brow. "You know, Jeff, I'm the committee representative to the board, and I always make a point to do that. But they've never provided us with an update for the newsletter," he said. Carolyn quickly chimed in, "I think the reason why we don't have as much about the junior high and high school is because we've had difficulty with getting teachers from each of the schools to be here at these meetings."

Jeff looked at both Randy and Carolyn for a few seconds before turning back to Stephanie. Glancing at his day-planner, he said, "Well, then, let's make sure to get you on the agenda for the next administrators' meeting. There's one coming up in two weeks, and that will give you some time with all three of us principals and the superintendent. I hate to put more work on my plate than I already have, but I'll get you an update for our building by May. Also, you're putting these newsletters up on the district's Web page too, right?"

Stephanie nodded affirmatively. "Great," Jeff said, making a note in his planner. "Now, remind me who is supposed to be here from the junior high again?"

"Um . . ." Stephanie thought for a minute. "Peggy from the physical education department was with us last year. And Bob from social studies has been here for a few meetings."

Jeff frowned. "Well, Peggy is out on maternity leave right now. I'll check with Bob. But I think it's important that we have at least two teachers from each school represented at these meetings."

Taking a deep breath, Stephanie said, "I think you're right, but we've had difficulties with getting them to commit to being here at every meeting. We have some time scheduled on the agenda today to talk about member recruitment and retention. I'd love to hear your thoughts about how we can improve this."

BRAINSTORMING FOR NEXT YEAR

Looking down at her agenda, Stephanie said, "It's already April, which is why I slated some time on the agenda to start discussing our goals for the next school year. We don't need to finalize these until June. But we should have a clear idea for what we want to accomplish by then so we can spend the summer months working on securing grant funding and planning for staffing in terms of interns and AmeriCorps volunteers. Right now, I just want do some brainstorming about the issues people are interested in addressing. Is there something specific we should start with?"

Carolyn said, "I think we should do something about the nutritional content of school meals. I stopped by the elementary school cafeteria this week and was really disappointed to see that they were serving hot dogs and chips for lunch. Hot dogs and chips! It doesn't get much worse than that!"

Randy nodded emphatically. "Julie has stopped in to have breakfast at the elementary school with the girls a couple of times and thinks it is just awful. The last time she was there, they were serving something that looked like lemon cake with icing. That's unacceptable. And she said that they offer cereals, but it's really sugary stuff like Frosted Flakes. How can we expect health and wellness policies to stick if this is what kids are eating in the schools?"

Jeff shook his head. "I know that one of the problems with the elementary school breakfast is the timing. Whatever they serve has to be fast because the younger children take a while to eat. There's not much time between when they are dropped off by the buses and when the bell rings. They really can't serve things like eggs there."

"Well, I'm sure there are lots of healthy grab-and-go type foods, though, that could be served," Kelly said. "What about Cheerios instead of Frosted Flakes?" Lauren, one of the AmeriCorps volunteers, offered. Amanda said, "Things like yogurt, and whole-wheat toast or a bagel would be a lot healthier, and just as quick as lemon cake."

A few committee members chuckled at Amanda's comment. Jeff sighed. "You're right. This is something I should bring up to Linda, the elementary principal, the next time I see her. The meals at the junior high are better because we have a cafeteria coordinator who plans our menus. The elementary school lost their coordinator in the fall, and I think the superintendent's office is filling in until they can find a replacement. But they just don't have time to do the job. In the meantime, I think addressing the nutritional content of the cafeteria menus is a big opportunity for this group. More than half of the kids in the district are eligible for free or reduced-priced lunches in the cafeterias. We want to be sure they're eating well so they're ready to learn."

Kelly offered, "One solution might be checking with Hickory Community College in West Oak. They have a fantastic dietetics program and their students are being trained in the economics of food, too. If the district can't find or afford another coordinator, we could look into creating an internship program for the dietetics students to partner with the school cooks to develop a healthier menu."

"That's a great idea," Stephanie said. Jeff abruptly interrupted, "Sure. But we do need to check whether the coordinator job is a union position. That was an issue a few years ago when we tried to limit the hours for the elementary and junior high's vending machines. The person who stocked the machines was a union member. It cut back on their job hours, and that was a big problem."

"That's right," Stephanie sighed. "It's the same issue we had with bringing in fresh fruit for a special breakfast promotion at the elementary school last spring. The cooks said they wouldn't have time to wash and cut up the fruit, and we can't add to their hours because of the union contract."

Randy snorted, "I think we might need to look into having someone from the union on the health committee, then."

Grimacing at the sarcasm in Randy's voice, Stephanie noticed Dan and Carolyn exchange a meaningful glance and look at Jeff, who was writing in his planner and appeared not to have heard the comment. As she started to suggest moving on to another issue, Kelly said, "You know, one way to get around that might be to reinforce that we're not selling the food, and since that doesn't affect the cafeteria workers, we should be able to bring someone else in to prep and hand out the fruit. That's what they do in the Elm Creek School District, at least."

Stephanie laughed. "If only we had the same resources as Elm Creek." Others around the room nodded emphatically. "So, it sounds like school lunch nutrition is definitely something we should have on the agenda for next year. Does anyone else have any ideas?"

KEY TERMS

brainstorming

group membership and boundaries

influences on group tasks and
    activities

leadership

meetings

power

roles

DISCUSSION QUESTIONS

1. How would you describe the boundaries of the Sycamore Schools Health Advisory Committee? In what ways could these boundaries function to help the group work effectively? In what ways could they function to hinder the group's ability to work effectively?

2. What kind of leadership style would you say Stephanie has been enacting? Has it been effective? Is there another style of leadership that might work better for this group?

3. Based on what you read, who do you think are the most powerful members of the group? Who might be the least powerful members? How do you know?

4. What sorts of factors seem to influence the members' status within the committee?

5. What kind of brainstorming technique did Stephanie use with the committee? Are there other techniques that you might recommend for this group given what you know about them?

DIFFERING VIEWPOINTS

Decision Making in a Nonprofit Meeting

Stephenson Beck and Joann Keyton

Employees of a growing nonprofit organization negotiate relationships and tasks related to a new project.

To many, Internet access is a natural part of life. Families without online computer access are considered to be disadvantaged or on the wrong side of the digital divide. That is where FreeInternet enters. FreeInternet is a nonprofit company that provides low-income families with computers and Internet access. They do this by selling Internet service to paying customers, with profits subsidizing low-income families' computer needs. FreeInternet also runs a community web page that highlights local events and opportunities for residents. FreeInternet found their niche in a college town of about eighty thousand. With more than two thousand subscribers, FreeInternet has helped thirty-five low-income families get Internet access in the last eighteen months.

Fred founded the company with the assistance of his girlfriend, Rita, and his good friend, Cal. Their initial office was in Fred's basement, but four months later they were able to rent a small office and warehouse space in a strip mall. Over the past year and a half their operation has grown from three to nine employees. With the additional hires, Fred has officially relinquished many of his original duties and now focuses his energy on recruiting new donors and improving overall marketing strategies.

Tom is the newest employee, hired three months ago. In his role as general manager, he coordinates the different entities of the company, especially as the team has been gearing up for the unveiling of a new server network, which will expand their wireless access across the entire city. Helping Tom in the office is Rita in finance, and Cal and Joe, who are both engineers. The rest of the staff includes Sarah (receptionist), Angie (clerk), and Dick and Pete (engineering assistants). Everyone spends most of the time in the office, except for the engineers and their assistants, who split their time between the office and on-site visits, and Fred, who is regularly out of the office. Sarah and Angie were hired five months ago, and they work part-time while attending a local university.

TOM'S MANAGEMENT CHALLENGE

Tom's first few days on the job were very pleasant, but as he began to take on the general manager role for the organization, he quickly became overwhelmed with juggling the day-to-day operations. He didn't lack ability; he had recently graduated from college and had two years' work experience with a local manufacturing company. He joined FreeInternet because he thought it was a worthy cause and liked the entrepreneurial spirit that Fred, Rita, and Cal had started. However, it became clear early on that Tom had his work cut out for him. When Fred added the general manager role, the organization had to reorganize who reported to whom, which required Tom to introduce some new operating procedures.

Clearly, Fred and Tom had different ways of doing things. Tom liked up-to-date reports and conversations with no beating around the bush. Tom also became frustrated when decisions and issues did not come directly through him. There had been a few bumps, especially when his blunt personality rubbed someone the wrong way. Despite these bumps, the group of workers generally met their deadlines and the organization continued to expand. From Tom's point of view, things were moving pretty smoothly toward the unveiling date of the new server network.

As part of his job, Tom started weekly meetings every Friday to coordinate work schedules among employees. Everyone was expected to attend the meetings, held first thing in the morning. Tom ran the meetings in a fairly informal style. At each meeting, he used the same procedure; he simply went around the room and asked for updates from each employee.

Tom is especially eager and anxious about the upcoming meeting as it is the last one before the big unveiling of the organization's new server, and he wants to make sure it goes well. Not only will having new server capacity increase their growth potential, but Tom wants to be successful in the company's first major decision and implementation since he took over as general manager. By the end of the meeting, he wants everyone to have a clear idea of what needs to be done for the upcoming week.

The Last Meeting Before the Unveiling

After greeting everyone, Tom begins the meeting by going over the upcoming week's schedule. He talks about each day in detail, highlighting the important points of the implementation. He repeats himself several times to make sure everyone is on the same page. This takes approximately twenty minutes. Following this, Tom returns to the standard procedure; he goes around the room, asking each team member to report on the past week. He starts with Rita.

"Hey, Rita, what have you been up to?"

"Well, we need to make a decision on whether to completely get rid of our old subscription and payment system, or to keep letting people use it," reports Rita. "We upgraded to a newer system last month, but people are still using the old system somewhat."

This last comment catches Tom by surprise. In a baffled voice, he inquires, "Are people really using the old system still? There can't be more than one . . ."

"Five people are," Rita interrupts.

"Really?" Tom scoffs.

"Really," responds Rita, whose tone of voice indicates that she is tired of this line of questioning.

"I don't get it," Tom says. "Why would someone keep using the old system when we have a better system?"

"Beats me," Cal chimes in.

"I don't know. But I've been thinking about it for a while, and I thought it would be better to bring it before you all before making a decision," says Rita. "This decision doesn't just affect me; it affects all of us. I didn't think it was fair for me to simply make the decision without receiving some input from everyone."

"I can't believe people are still using it," Tom mutters loudly to himself.

After a pause, Fred speaks for the first time all meeting. "Why don't we just stop adding people to it?"

"That's what I was kinda thinking," Rita adds quickly.

Fred turns to the engineers. "Cal and Joe, that means your paperwork is going to change. And Angie, you will really need to keep up-to-date on those files from the new system."

"What about people who still want to use it?" Tom blurts out. "What about little old Miss Hatfield who pays her bill through the old system? We are abandoning her."

"That is why we will continue to have it up, but we just won't add anyone new so it will slowly phase out," Rita says matter-of-factly.

"After a while, we'll formally close it," adds Angie.

"Sounds like a good idea," says Joe.

"Yep," agrees Cal.

Clearing his throat, Tom speaks. "Well, okay, then let's make it official—no new people will be added to the system. Many of you will need to change how you do things." Tom then comments on several changes staff members will need to make as a result of this decision.

After Rita's turn ends, Tom continues going around the room, asking everyone to report on the past week and his or her plans for the unveiling. He finishes up by inquiring about

Fred's efforts over the past week. Fred pretends not to hear the initial question, prompting Tom to ask again.

"So what have you been up to, Fred?"

Looking up, Fred says in a very casual tone, "Oh, nothing. Just surfing the Internet." It's clear Fred is not accustomed to be questioned in this way.

Cal, Joe, and Rita giggle at Fred's comment. Since his comment has the intended effect, Fred continues.

"I was thinking about buying a new weight set, you know, just to play around with. And I was checking out some fun YouTube videos of people falling off ladders."

"Sounds busy," Tom interjects, with a laugh that seems a little artificial.

"Yeah, well, you know." Fred then sits up, looks everyone in the eye, and speaks in a much stronger voice. "Actually, I just want everyone to know what an important week this is for us. First of all, on Monday . . ."

Fred then speaks for fifteen minutes discussing the upcoming week's schedule, emphasizing the importance of what they are doing, and making sure everyone is on top of their assignments. He touches on many similar points that Tom has already mentioned, including confirming their decision on the old subscription and payment system. Following his comments, Fred leaves, indicating that he has a meeting scheduled with another potential donor. Then Tom adjourns the meeting.

MEETING AFTERMATH

Later that day, Cal, Joe, and Pete are working onsite. They like working together and regularly discuss a variety of issues, from sports to politics to religion. When someone mentions how they like to kill time watching NASCAR, Cal moves back to a discussion about the meeting earlier that day.

"Speaking of killing time, that sure was another boring meeting. I'm glad they only happen once a week. More than that would probably put me to sleep."

"Seriously," agrees Joe. "Like that discussion about the payment plan. Why do we need to sit there every week and watch Tom and Rita go at it? Every week it is the same thing— they fight like cat and mouse."

"Were they fighting?" Pete asks. "Does that happen a lot?"

"All the time, fighting just like they did in the meeting," laughs Cal. "Tom tries to show that he is in charge, and Rita just likes to bug him. She brings up issues that he knows nothing about just to see him get all worked up. They've always kinda hated each other. They bicker the whole time, him wanting to always be in control, and her always showing him that he isn't all high and mighty."

"And then Fred straightens him out. Which is why I can't stand those meetings," scowls Joe. "If they are going to simply make the decision without discussion, then why bring it before us? Why do we have to be there?"

"Isn't Tom supposed to make decisions like that? I thought that was his job," Pete asks.

"Oh, it doesn't matter what the job description says, Fred is always going to make the decision without getting anyone's advice," sighs Cal. "That is just the way it is."

"Unless of course Rita *talks* to him later," Joe says, winking.

A FEW HOURS LATER

At the end of the day, Tom and Rita are alone working in the office. Tom has been looking for an opportunity to talk with her all day. Rita has been in meetings, but when the last person finally leaves the office, she leans back in her chair and lets out a big sigh. Tom takes this moment to poke his head in the door.

"Hey, Rita, sounds like you've had a pretty busy day."

"Pretty nonstop," Rita says, tiredly. "Preparing for this unveiling has been all I've been doing for the past three weeks. I can't wait until it is here."

"I hear you. It has been difficult to keep everything coordinated, and we've had quite a few big decisions to make," Tom says. After a pause, he continues, "By the way, how do you think everything has been running?"

"Same old, same old."

"Yeah, I think it has been going pretty well, too," Tom says, with a smile. "Everyone seems to be pretty excited about the big unveiling, and I can sense Fred is happy with how we've come together. Also, I thought we had a good discussion today about the new subscription and payment system."

"It was good to get out our opinions and for us to collectively make the best decision. I think it was important that we were all involved since it influenced all of us," says Rita, yawning distractedly.

"Yeah, it is always helpful to ask questions and clarify things. That's why I think we work well together; we make sure that we are committed to a choice before deciding on a solution," Tom says.

"Absolutely," Rita quickly agrees. "I think you and I do a pretty good job of fleshing out issues. I think our thoughtful approach to each issue benefits the organization, and others realize that. In fact, sometimes I think if we didn't discuss issues, then everyone would be at a loss for what to do."

"Exactly," says Tom.

"Well, I have to go. Meeting with Fred for our Friday night date. Hopefully he won't bore me with more work talk. He always tells me about what he thinks about everything happening in the office, and he always wants my opinions. I wish we could just let work go and enjoy ourselves, instead of making important decisions during our date. Gotta go. See ya."

"Bye."

Tom watches as Rita leaves. He stands there thinking for a moment, before slowly heading back to his office, head bowed.

KEY TERMS

communication climate	power
conflict styles	roles
decision making	task and relational communication
leadership	

DISCUSSION QUESTIONS

1. Why do Cal and Joe have such different versions of the subscription and payment system discussion than Tom and Rita? Did you think that Tom and Rita were fighting before reading Cal and Joe's comments?

2. How does the organizational or meeting context influence how the different members interpreted the meeting interaction?

3. Which group members' contributions were influential to making a decision about the new subscription and payment system? Were all group members' messages necessary?

4. How would you describe the communication climate present in the meeting? How do you know this?

5. Who is the leader of the meeting? On what basis did you make that identification?

6. How was power manifest in the meeting? Who held what type of power?

7. What steps could be taken to improve the meetings?

BUSINESS PROCESS MODELING AT THE INTERNAL FUNDING OFFICE

Structuring Group Interaction to Structure Business Processes

Logan Franken and David R. Seibold

Members of a group within the Internal Funding Office of a small governmental organization work to create a comprehensive document of business activities.

"All right, let's get started," Diane said as she leaned back in her chair and closed the door to the Internal Funding Office's conference room. This was going to be a challenge, she thought. Her team was tasked with documenting *all* of the business processes at the Internal Funding Office, a time-consuming and tedious job and one to which individual members of the team had different levels of commitment. What would be needed for the group to succeed? She glanced around the room at the usual group members seated around the table, and then turned toward the two newcomers seated against the wall. "Welcome to our business process modeling group. I'll start by explaining a little bit about what we do."

The Internal Funding Office (IFO) is a small branch, consisting of only forty employees, within a major state-funded institution. The unit administers and manages state and government finances for various programs throughout the organization. About a year ago, the IFO started a new initiative called business process modeling. Business process modeling refers to the creation of documents that comprehensively describe an organization's business processes. These business processes can range from minor and routine activities, such as dealing with external requests for information, to major and vital events, such as establishing a legal contract with a new client. Although business process modeling generally refers to the creation of graphical flowcharts that depict activities within a given business process, business process modeling also can refer simply to writing textual descriptions of processes.

The IFO began business process modeling for two principal reasons. First, the unit's internal software developers needed to rebuild the software application used within many of the IFO's core processes. For many years, the unit had depended on a software application provided by the federal government, extending and modifying the application to fit their needs. However, the federal government decided to drop its support for the program, forcing the IFO's software developers to upgrade their ad hoc extensions into a full-fledged replacement application. As a result, there was a need for clear documentation of current processes to guide the design and development of such an application.

Second, many of the staff members who had worked at the IFO for extensive periods of time were nearing retirement. These employees had developed a deep understanding of the unit's daily activities, but not all of this knowledge was explicitly documented. In fact, some of this information was only known to the employees themselves. With these employees nearing retirement, the IFO required a method for capturing and retaining this valuable knowledge.

The IFO had attempted a similar imitative several years ago. They hired a writer from outside the unit to interview all the employees about their business processes and translate this information into a comprehensive volume. This was a response to a requirement from the federal government that the IFO should document all of its business practices. Unfortunately, since the business activities of the IFO change constantly in response to bureaucratic policy modifications and fiscal constraints, the writer's documentation was outdated by the time she completed the interviews. Furthermore, since the writer lacked the staff's extensive experience with the business processes, she had a difficult time developing a complete understanding of every process. The documentation consequently lacked depth and contained numerous errors.

Learning from those experiences, the IFO decided to have the staff write the documentation themselves rather than depend on someone from outside the organization. When the business process modeling initiative began, the unit managers asked individual staff members to document specific processes. This involved writing an extensive explanation of all the steps involved within a given process. After completing a draft of the documentation, each staff member would bring a copy to a meeting with the managers, who would critique it. This approach proved overly formal, however. As one staff member remarked, "It was all managers, and it felt like they were attacking."

So the IFO implemented a new strategy for business process modeling. Staff members were split into three groups of five to six members. Members of management that were intimately involved in the unit's daily business practices were also added to these groups. Each group member was tasked with modeling one or more business processes based on their personal expertise. Similar to the original meetings, staff members would bring a draft of their business process documentation to the meetings, read it aloud, and listen to critiques and suggestions from fellow group members. Staff members felt more comfortable in this informal group setting because they were surrounded by their peers.

Business process modeling drafts were written in a narrative format and had three parts: a timeline, a table of contents, and a story. The timeline and table of contents were general overviews of the major phases within a process, while the stories were detailed descriptions of a given business process from start to finish. Although each group planned on meeting weekly, the groups met more sporadically: One group met every other week while another group met less than once a month. Diane's group, however, met on a weekly basis.

Diane turned toward Mark, another group member, and suggested, "Let's start with the ALPHA program." Mark nodded, and Diane slid the wireless keyboard and mouse over to his seat at the table. The other group members watched as Mark moved the mouse around on the projected computer screen and navigated to the directory where the business process modeling documentation was stored. When he attempted to open one of the files, however, the computer froze.

"It's thinking," Mark joked as he impatiently wiggled the mouse back and forth. The other group members laughed and Rebecca, a group member, added, "It's slower than usual." Diane agreed, "It is, that's true. Wow." After a minute of silence, the computer began responding again and Mark opened the timeline, table of contents, and storyline for his program, the ALPHA program. Mark began, "All right, I'll start with the table of contents."

Diane leaned back and narrowed her eyes in concentration. As one of the IFO's managers, she strongly supported the business process modeling initiative. She worked at the IFO when they had hired the writer to document the processes, so she understood the importance of culling knowledge directly from staff members. In fact, her favorite aspect of the initiative was the collaboration between staff members: She saw business process modeling as a learning opportunity, where each group member learned about one another's programs and also discovered the ways in which members of the staff intricately depend upon each other. Although she admitted that writing and reading through the lengthy documentation was a tedious process, both for her and her fellow group members, she was emphatically committed to business process modeling. She saw the initiative as a stepping-stone that would allow the IFO to evolve as an organization.

Mark finished reading the table of contents and opened the ALPHA program timeline. He explained, "Here's my timeline, based on Rebecca's template. So, for January . . ."

While Mark was reading, Rebecca leaned forward and scanned the text. As the data operations manager, Rebecca handled the majority of the daily operations related to retrieving the data used within the IFO's core software application. Consequently, many of the unit's business processes depended on reports and updates generated directly by her. Given Rebecca's ubiquitous responsibilities, she not only led her own business process modeling meeting, but she also attended all of the other modeling meetings as well. Although she strongly supported business process modeling and saw the initiative as a critical necessity, she bemoaned the amount of time required to document each of the processes. Writing the business process modeling documentation was another "to do" in her typically frenzied schedule of responsibilities, and she wished that she had more time.

Mark continued, "In October, I verify that we have received all of the ALPHA Funding Agreements. There are so few of these that I have been keeping track of them manually."

Rebecca interjected, "Do we need to put in a check for the ALPHA Funding Agreements? We don't want the funds to disburse without the Funding Agreement, right?"

"Yeah," Mark replied, "I think we need to change that because last year they didn't have a Funding Agreement online and now they do. This year, I don't know that the regulations say they have to do the online Funding Agreement, because they were able to complete it in person before."

"Now that we have the online Funding Agreement," Diane explained, "we will no longer do it in person."

"So we should be checking prior to disbursement that it's completed," Rebecca added.

"Right," Mark agreed. He continued reading through the timeline, and then opened the story for the ALPHA program. "So, the story . . ."

Mark began reading the story aloud to the rest of the group members. Although Mark was committed to accurately documenting his process, he distrusted the motivation for the initiative. He believed that the IFO began business process modeling in response to budgetary constraints: If they had the funds, then they could simply purchase a thoroughly tested software application from an outside vendor rather than force the IFO's software developers to hurriedly develop a replacement. As he saw it, the IFO lacked sufficient funding due to the state government's mismanagement of fiscal surpluses: The unit was forced to spend yearly surpluses rather than save the funds for later purchases. Despite his suspicions, Mark agreed that business process modeling was a viable tool for documenting business activities. Furthermore, he respected his fellow group members and was committed to completing his documentation for the common good of the group.

The group members listened as Mark continued reading, "Then I get a report from Rebecca . . ."

Rebecca suggested, "That should be data operations manager, because you don't want to change it when I retire in four months."

Mark responded, "Geez, four months? That's too soon. All right, let me change that." He edited the text onscreen and continued, "So, back to the story . . ."

Kenneth sat straight up in his chair and read through the text, looking for errors in punctuation and spelling. Kenneth did not feel as committed to business process modeling as did the rest of his group members because his programs were relatively small and uncomplicated business practices. He had recently been promoted to a management position, so he was given less responsibility in business process modeling in order to compensate for his increased responsibilities as a new manager. Like his fellow group members, he found the process of reading and writing the documentation tedious and time-consuming. However, despite feeling relatively uncommitted, he saw business process modeling as a valuable initiative, particularly for its potential to provide the software developers with a guide for developing their new application.

Kenneth spoke up. "I think you meant 'recipients,' plural, instead of 'recipient.'"

"Yeah, you're right," Mark smiled. "You always catch my grammatical mistakes." He fixed the error and continued, "So, in June I send an e-mail out to all of the ALPHA program recipients, requesting that they renew their Funding Agreement for the following year."

Margaret broke in, "Do you send out the same e-mail to each recipient?"

"No," Mark answered, "we send out different e-mails depending on . . ."

Margaret leaned forward and rested her clipboard against the table as she listened to Mark's response. As the head of the IFO's internal software development team, she was always conceptualizing how the various business processes could be represented in computer code. Margaret strongly supported the business process modeling initiative. In fact, she was the person who originally suggested business process modeling to the managers of the IFO. For her, business process modeling was first and foremost a tool for gathering and organizing knowledge to develop the IFO's replacement software application.

Rebecca suggested, "You should probably include a copy of those e-mails."

"Yep," Mark agreed and typed in a reminder amid the text. "Actually, I was wondering about that. Margaret, are these e-mails included as part of the actual models?"

"No, not directly. When my team creates the graphical models, we'll probably add 'Send e-mails' as a step within the business process, but we won't include the full text of the actual e-mail. That reminds me: Are we going to keep sending these e-mails, because I know it was different before. Right, Linda?"

Linda nodded, "Yeah, we used to . . ."

Linda had worked in the IFO for over ten years. She managed several programs during her years at the IFO, including the ALPHA program. Like many of her fellow group members, she disliked the tedious and time-consuming process of writing out every minute detail of her daily business activities. However, she recognized the valuable potential of business process modeling as an instructional aide for new employees. When she originally took over her primary responsibility, the BETA program, there was little documentation explaining the various duties of her new position. Most of the documentation that did exist was outdated. She was forced to arduously relearn the intuitive, tacit knowledge known only to the person previously in her position. As a result, she saw business process modeling as an invaluable resource for both new staff members and current staff members shifting into new positions.

Despite her positive assessment of business process modeling, she remembered her initial apprehension toward the initiative. She was among the first staff members asked to model her business process, and when Margaret presented an example of a finished graphical model it was a little overwhelming. How would she translate a business process that she personally understood into an explicit technical model that could be used for developing a software application? The task seemed daunting. Margaret reassured her, however, that the team of developers would create the actual graphical models and that the staff would instead write the textual descriptions, or "stories," of the processes. This notion of a "story" seemed to make the task of business process modeling more manageable for Linda. She thought the narrative format was a nice alternative to the rigid, flat tone of most instructional texts.

Mark reached the end of his story and jokingly remarked, "The end!" Diane smiled and replied, "Thank you." She looked at the clock displayed in the corner of the projected computer screen and decided it was time to conclude the meeting. "Okay, let's stop here. For next week, Mark, can you make those changes?"

"Sure," Mark agreed.

"Okay, great, so we'll review those changes and then we'll begin reviewing the BETA program. Does that sound okay?"

The group members nodded.

"After that, we will only have two more programs to go, so my hope is that we'll be finished in three weeks. Great work, everyone, thank you!"

As the group members filed out of the conference room, Diane turned off the computer and returned to her office. She sat at her desk and looked out the window, thinking about her group's progress in business process modeling. Diane sensed that the group members had varying levels of commitment to business process modeling, and she knew almost everyone disliked the tedium of the process, but they were still successfully completing the documentation. "Probably because they are able to talk so openly with each other," Diane thought to herself. Her mouth formed a wry and knowing smile as she considered a compelling aspect of these meetings: Despite their differing commitments to the initiative and their personal feelings about the tedium of business process modeling, members' interactions with each other during the group's meetings were just as important as the processes that they were modeling. In turn, the quality of those interactions—especially how the members were using communication to structure themselves in order to accomplish the task—was leading to the group's success at structuring the larger work processes.

KEY TERMS

business process modeling	leadership
conflict	nonverbal behaviors
group outcomes	structuration theory
group structure	technology
influences on group tasks and activities	

DISCUSSION QUESTIONS

1. Compare the three different approaches to documenting business processes at IFO. Why were the first two not as successful as the third approach?

2. Compare and contrast each member's perspective on business process modeling and understanding of the motivations behind the initiative. What factors led to their divergent viewpoints?

3. How would you characterize the nature of communication in the group? What effects, if any, did the group's interaction patterns have in facilitating business process modeling?

4. How do the non-verbal behaviors of the group members, including their seating arrangements, symbolize their different perspectives on business process modeling?

5. Is leadership limited to one member or is there more than one group leader? What effect does this have on participation and group interaction in the meeting?

6. How does the changing nature of IFO's work impact business process modeling?

7. How does technology both constrain and enable the business process modeling activities of the group?

UNPREPARED FOR THE PREPAREDNESS GROUP

Anticipatory Socialization, Entry, and Assimilation into an Intact Workgroup

Leah M. Omilion

A hospital's emergency preparedness team is accepting a new member, yet not until she can prove her abilities to the group.

Marie sat in her office shifting her weight as she rotated from side to side in her chair, anxiously watching the clock on the bottom right-hand side of her screen. She gathered her papers—still grouped together in the same manner as they had been ten minutes earlier—and resorted them, pressed them against her chest, and sighed.

"What am I going to do in *that* group?" Marie thought. "If Pam didn't have such a big mouth, I wouldn't be in this position."

Marie thought back to the moment when Pam had told her that she would be joining the hospital's Emergency Preparedness group. As the Chief Marketing Officer, Pam had just come back from a Senior Leadership meeting and was excited, proud even, to show the organization Marie's advanced academic skills and the depth of the Marketing Department. She thought it would help Marie advance in the organization and grow personally, not to mention the prestige it would bring to the department. The Senior Leadership team thought that it was essential that the group have a communication expert, "and who better than Marie?" thought Pam.

"This will move you up to the next level. You know who's in that group, all of the decision makers—it'll be good for them to see how smart you are. You can show them what a good job we do in marketing, too," gushed Pam.

The Emergency Preparedness group was a highly specialized assembly composed of members from all the major departments of the hospital. Human Resources, Emergency,

Infection Control, Employee Health, Rehabilitation, Dietary, Building and Grounds, and Laboratory were just a few of the departments that had a representative in the group. With each department sending their most knowledgeable member, the Emergency Preparedness group was well equipped to ensure that the hospital was in capable hands in case of crisis.

"She's a good boss," Marie thought, "but sometimes, she oversteps her boundaries." While Pam knew that Marie was going to graduate school in the evenings for communication and that she had taken courses in crisis management, she neglected to consider that there may be notable differences between textbooks about crisis and joining the hospital's long-standing, award-winning Emergency Preparedness group.

EARLY EXPERIENCES WITH THE EMERGENCY PREPAREDNESS GROUP

Marie didn't know much about the Emergency Preparedness group, but like other exclusive groups, there was room to speculate. "Why do they always walk around here so quickly? Why do they look so secretive? Who do they think they are, the CIA?"

The only firsthand experience Marie had had with the group was when she was in a meeting in the large boardroom a year prior. It was a typical Wednesday afternoon and Marie was in the middle of meeting with the orthopedic team, when the Emergency Preparedness group burst in without so much as a knock and began to rifle through cabinets, hurriedly pulling out booklets, walkie talkies, and vests. There were six of them at that point; however, within minutes an additional five walked through the door and aided in establishing the "Command Center." Even at the time, Marie thought, "Command Center? How pretentious."

Marie sat in astonishment along with the orthopedic team. The hospital subscribed to the traditional physician-centered operating model. As such, the director of orthopedics was offended by the group's lack of respect for his meeting and went directly to the president and CEO, ordering the remainder of meeting attendees to "stay put."

Moments later Bill, the president and CEO, came in and while he apologized for the truncated meeting, told them that the Emergency Preparedness group had a mandatory simulation and the large boardroom was designated as Command Center. Marie was surprised that the doctors' wishes were relegated beneath this other group's. That was not the way the hospital worked.

"Yup, that's the standard operating procedure—SOP," said one of the group members. She was wearing a fluorescent orange vest that had "COMMANDER" written across the chest and stamped on the back. "Bill, you know the drill. Get 'em all out of here, you're hurting our time and right now we have the best record of any group in the state. Now. I mean it," she continued.

Marie couldn't believe that anyone would speak like that to Bill. Not only was he the organization's leader, but he was also a strict, no-nonsense type of man. Marie anticipated that he'd ask the woman to accompany him out of the conference room and into his office. Instead, Bill simply said, "You're right, Nancy. We're all leaving. Keep up the good work."

"Nancy, you're right?!" thought Marie to herself. "Who is this woman, and what is it that she and this group do that allows them so much latitude?"

After that event, Marie began to see some of the group members around the hospital. They always walked in groups and did so quickly, close to one another, and frequently spoke in whispers. Marie didn't know their names. She'd try to look at their ID badges as they passed, but it was clear from the faded, splotchy images and ill-defined letters on the badges that they had been organizational members for many years. There was Nancy, of course, and a tall, thin man with salt and pepper hair and a matching mustache who also accompanied her. Many times, a shorter, stout, balding man would round out the pair.

However, aside from the occasional curiosity piqued by seeing one of the members in the hallways, Marie did not think or hear of the group. That is, until the day that Marie's boss told her that she was a member.

MARIE'S FIRST MEETING

The clock at the bottom of the screen displayed "11:00 AM," indicating that it was time for her to attend her first meeting as a member. Marie took the stairs, all four flights, to delay her arrival at the meeting. It was not that Marie was unpunctual or trying to be late, but the culture of the hospital was that meetings typically ran five minutes later than was scheduled to make up for the five minutes they were delayed by the previous group. Instead of sitting awkwardly with the group members before their meeting, Marie preferred to take her time to avoid the situation.

When she arrived at Room D, there was no one waiting in the hallway. Thinking that she had mistaken the time or location due to her nerves, she called her assistant to confirm. Laura, her assistant, answered immediately and upon recognizing Marie's voice responded, "Are they that bad, you've already left?"

"No, I haven't left yet. I haven't even arrived. Can you check and let me know when and where the meeting is?"

Moments later, Laura confirmed what Marie had feared; despite the fact that all meetings unofficially began five minutes late, the Emergency Preparedness group began on time.

"Oh, boy. This is not going to be good. Wish me luck," said Marie before hanging up the phone.

Marie stood outside Room D for a few moments deciding whether she should knock. She could hear that they were in discussion and thought it'd be less distracting if she were to simply walk in. As she entered, a silence fell upon the room. Ten of the people she had watched in the Command Center a year earlier now all watched her. All but one had turned to examine her. She recognized Nancy's short dark hair from behind and that matter-of-fact tone.

"We start at 11:00, not 11:03. Sit down," ordered Nancy.

Marie looked around the U-shaped table for a vacant seat. As she approached it, the woman sitting on one side moved her binder over and said that it was taken. Not thinking much of it, Marie moved a few feet over to take another seat. The man next to the chair put his coffee mug in front of it indicating that it too was reserved. Annoyed, Marie walked over to the opposite side of the table where she encountered the same treatment.

The meeting still had not resumed, with all members' eyes fixed on her. She thought that she could walk out and no "normal" person would blame her for abandoning the situation. However, there was something about this exclusive group, perhaps their prestige, their rules, even their overtly rude verbal and nonverbal communication behaviors that compelled her to stay for at least one meeting. Her position in the Marketing Department allowed her the rare privilege of possessing a hospital skeleton key. She was confident that she was the only one in the room with one, which also allowed her to access the locked closet door. She used the key that she carried on the back side of her badge to open the closet of the conference room and get herself a chair.

"Don't worry about not having enough chairs. I brought my own," Marie said as she sat down. She was irritated by their discourteous treatment, but intrigued by the group. While many of the members let out audible sighs and others rolled their eyes, she saw a slight smirk run across Nancy's face.

The meeting proceeded as most do; there was an agenda and Nancy led the group through it. The lanky man who was always at Nancy's side, Sam, was in charge of being the time-keeper, and the short man, Don, recorded the meetings. Sam was conscientious—Marie watched him as he helped to lead the meetings with Nancy. He'd constantly refer to his computer for the information that had escaped the group while simultaneously monitoring his watch, doing his part to keep the group on task. Don, more reserved than Nancy and Sam, was methodical. He transcribed the meeting the same way that a recorder captures voices, in whole, even noting when a speaker's tone or pitch deviated from what was expected. While Nancy was clearly the leader, it was equally evident that she, Sam, and Don composed the heart of the group, accounting for all group occurrences, industry updates, and strategic planning.

The way that this meeting differed from all others that Marie attended was in content. They discussed possible biochemical, nuclear, or firearm attacks and then planned for the disaster. One member proposed teaching a seminar on identifying various skin lesions ranging from those incurred from chemical attacks to those characteristic of the plague. Another member argued that it was necessary to reconsider the hospital's backup plan in case the morgue was at capacity due to disaster. Marie sat through the meeting and took notes. The notes were not made as a reference to which she would like to return, but rather occupied her so that she did not focus too intently on the topics at hand. She also began to jot down some notes that would allow her to introduce herself properly to the group, some facts that would help her to establish credibility. She would talk about her master's degree and about her experience as a doctoral student. As the meeting drew to a close, Marie stood to introduce herself. After "Hi, my name is Marie," the members gathered their belongings and began to file out the door.

"They're not ready to know you," said Nancy as Marie was leaving the meeting. "We don't know if you're going to cut it."

There was never any mention of a tryout, thought Marie. "What can someone do for this group to accept them?" wondered Marie.

FITTING IN?

Since they provided Marie no responsibility and hence, no assignments, she had no interaction with the group until the next meeting two weeks later. She purposefully arrived early, and to her surprise found all the members sitting on one side of the U-shaped table, with one chair residing at the opposite, empty side. She took her place and again, the meeting proceeded as it would normally if she were not present.

"They'll tolerate me because Senior Leadership told them they had to, but that does not mean that they have to include me," Marie concluded.

This trend continued for several months. Instead of the routine meeting, one day Nancy said that the group needed to practice putting on their personal protective equipment (PPE). Marie had never seen anything like it in real life. "Wow! This looks like the suits that spacemen wear on TV and in the movies," thought Marie.

After a brief introduction of how to properly assemble the PPE, Nancy informed the group that everyone would need a partner as the final step required someone to duct tape the suit to protect the person wearing it from harmful outside particles. Additionally, the suits weighed approximately twenty pounds apiece, were difficult to maneuver, and required the individual to follow a series of intricate steps to assemble it properly.

"Don't worry, Marie. We don't expect you to do this. Especially since you're dressed inappropriately," said Sam.

Her position in the Marketing Department required her to attend many meetings, events, and work with the press. For these reasons, she dressed in a professional manner. However, due to their positions, many of the other Emergency Preparedness members were able to wear scrubs or jeans. Marie looked at her skirt and thought, "I am going to get into that suit if it kills me."

No one volunteered to work with Marie; instead there were several groups of two, and one group of three. However, she gathered her suit and followed the instructions that were provided by Nancy. Step by step, she worked quickly and was the first member to finish the task, save the final portion that required the help of a partner. Nancy brought this to the attention of the group.

"Well, look what we have here," Nancy said with a slight laugh. "Marie has her suit on first and she's done it correctly and without a partner. Even with those high heels on, she beat the rest of you." Marie left the training session feeling triumphant. As she left the room and traversed the hallways back to her office, two of the group members approached her.

"Wow! I don't know how you did that! I couldn't even walk in those shoes, let alone assemble the suit in them. I'm Kathy, by the way," she continued, "And this is Rebecca from Employee Health, oh, and I'm from Rehab."

Marie didn't know how to respond. She had sat across from these women for months and had not received so much as a nod of acknowledgement. Her initial response was to walk away, to return the ill treatment they had bestowed upon her earlier. However, she realized that this was an opportunity to begin to integrate into this group.

"Thanks, it's all in a day's work," said Marie as she smiled at each of the women and extended her hand. "Marie from Marketing, nice to meet you."

At the next meeting, the chairs were arranged in a normal spacing around the table and for the first time Marie was invited to sit among the members of the group.

While Marie was included more than she had been previously, she still felt like an outsider. She had not received any responsibilities despite the fact that she had been a member for nearly a year. Nancy, passing her in the hall one afternoon, pulled Marie aside and told her that the group had a difficult time letting others in. The group was highly specialized and had had a few new members in previous years, but after spending considerable time training them, they left.

"It's not a job for just anyone. It's a great responsibility to keep everyone—employees, patients and visitors—safe in the case of an emergency. We can't let just *anyone* in, but you're doing well. Sam even mentioned that it may be prudent for you to teach us how we should respond to the media in the event of a disaster," said Nancy as she walked away. Before she turned, she had smiled and winked at Marie and Marie smiled in return, acknowledging that she understood Nancy's message.

"It's not that they are mean, they just care so deeply about the safety of everyone around them that they need to make sure that they can trust me and that I too am invested in the cause," Marie realized finally.

Marie admired the group and knew that they worked well together. At times they were like a well-oiled machine. Marie found it difficult to tell where one group member's work had ended and another had picked up the project. She came to respect the members for their expertise—each major department of the hospital had a representative within the group— and despite Marie, all had elected to send the member that had the longest tenure. Many of the members had been with the organization for decades, whereas Marie had been hired just two years earlier. Additionally, Marie was significantly younger than the other members, gathering from the conversations they shared with each other that she was most likely closer in age to their children than to the group members themselves.

Despite her age and recent entry into the organization, Marie was well educated (a bachelor's degree in writing and public relations, a master's degree in public relations and communication, and progressing on a PhD in communication) and had previous experience within organizations that allowed her to work closely with multiple stakeholders including extensive work with the press. Pam had told her that she was "a little different from what we typically hire, but I have a good feeling about you."

CRISIS MODE AT COMMAND CENTER

It was this previous experience and educational background that allowed her to become a "full" member of the Emergency Preparedness group. It was a blustery winter day in the Midwest, one that required numerous local school districts to close for boiler issues or questions regarding the safety of busing children to school along the icy roads. Marie worked the early shift (6 a.m.—3 p.m.), and was surprised when her emergency pager went off as she was driving in. Pulling over, she saw the following page, "Command Center established. Water main break, no water. Report immediately."

Marie's mind was flooded with thoughts and anxiety. What would she be asked to do? Would she be able to do it?

When she arrived in the Command Center, the same boardroom she had been kicked out of previously, Nancy handed her an orange vest that read, "PUBLIC INFORMATION OFFICER." "This is you, kid. You're going to do great."

Marie was shocked by the comment and found herself shaking her head as she walked to the large table, finding a place to set up her laptop. Nancy went over the schedule of events again. "At oh five hundred hours, the main water line in the city broke. Initially the service folks told us it'd be repaired within the hour. However, the extreme temperatures caused a greater break when they tried to fix it. The hospital is without running water. This means that drinking fountains are hazardous, people can't use the sinks to wash their hands, and toilets can't flush. What are we going to do?"

While the team knew the logistics of the building and the technical problems associated with the water main break, it was Marie's strong grasp of communication and her place within the Marketing Department that allowed the Emergency Preparedness Group to succeed.

"First we need to create signs for the drinking fountains and restrooms. I will have my colleagues in Marketing make them now. Second, we need to communicate a message immediately to all employees so that they may help us in informing patients and visitors of the special circumstances. I'll make a talking points sheet so that everyone is using a message that we approve."

Marie then created a press release to preempt the local media's coverage of the story. She was able to communicate that the water main break was no fault of the hospital's and emphasize the proactive measures in place that allowed the hospital to continue to provide exceptional service to patients, guests, and the local community.

The other group members succeeded in carrying out their responsibilities; assessing the hospital's census, discussing methods to distribute water, investigating concerns of emergency surgeries under such conditions. After seven hours of crisis, the local agency was able to repair the water main and restore the hospital to normalcy.

As the Command Center disbanded, Marie slowly closed up her laptop, taking time to wrap up the power cord carefully. She was exhausted, but felt proud. After she secured her computer and other materials in her bag, she began to help the group members disband the phones, fold up the vests, and charge the walkie talkies. Nancy was providing an overview of the events and planning ahead for the after-action meeting that would occur sometime within the next 48 hours. Before she dismissed the group, she took a few minutes to recognize Marie for her "exemplary poise and strength under pressure."

"It's been a long time since we had a new member, and then one that stayed. It's not an easy job, being a part of this team and training yourself to always think of the worst case scenario, but it's a vital one. Kathy, over there, is our newest member before you and she's been with us for six years. We were tough on you, and you stuck around and showed that we can not only trust you, but depend on you. Welcome to the team, Newbie."

At this point, assorted members of the team came to congratulate Marie, apologize for their previous actions, and commend her on her work of the day. As she went to leave the Command Center, she heard Nancy yell, "And will you stop calling it the Emergency Preparedness Group already? We're the E-Prep team."

KEY TERMS

conflict	leadership
group development	norms
group identity	roles

DISCUSSION QUESTIONS

1. Despite being initially excluded, Marie still demonstrated a strong need to belong to the Emergency Preparedness group. Why do you believe that Marie was attracted to this group? Discuss how she moved from isolation to inclusion. Also consider how Marie shifted her perspective from individualism to collectivism.

2. The case study presents several instances of group conflict. Select a particular instance (i.e., initial meeting, personal protective equipment training, and subsequent meetings) and discuss conflict management styles that were evident in that instance. What conflict management styles and tactics could have helped the group members to better manage the situation?

3. Marie had a difficult time assimilating into the Emergency Preparedness group. Discuss ways in which she could have made her integration more

seamless. Be sure to incorporate group identity, norms and group development into your response.

4. Group members' actions and behaviors are shaped by the group's norms. What are the norms of the Emergency Preparedness group? Discuss verbal, nonverbal and other behavioral norms that are present in the case. After assessing the group's norms, discuss how they affect the group's identity. You may wish to consider how group members see the group and how non-group members view the group.

1) In the begining of the case study, Marie went into her first meeting with a bad attitude toward Pam, & was confused. Could this be some of the reasons why she got shit?

2) Marie has a very determined attitude throughout the time working in "E-prep" could she have done anything more to gain a greater amount of respect?

3) 6 years is a long time to be Joying to be in a group & not techniquelly accepted. How would you react to wear maria was if you were in her shoes at the 1yr, 3yr, 6yr?

4) Recall Marie's memory with the CEO & the E-prep team. Could she have spoke up at that moment and asked why? would this hurt or harm her. in her future with E-prep

5) What does the last sentence " and will you stop calling it ..... were the E-prep team" mean to you & significantly?

PART *Group Development, Roles, and Norms*

case 5

"HAVING WHAT IT TAKES"

A Collegiate Forensics Team's Business Meetings

Annette N. Hamel

A newcomer tries to adapt to the pressures of participating in a successful speech and debate team.

"Okay, everybody, meeting time! Let's go!" Ellen Redman called to the members of Middlebrook College's speech team as they laughed and joked in the "bull pen," the classroom where they gathered to study and rehearse their speech events. She jangled the keys to the classroom across the hall, where the team's weekly business meetings were held. Ellen was the faculty member at Middlebrook who coached the speech team, planning the events and accompanying the students to tournaments, and she was rarely in the mood for nonsense or delays. Her students looked up to her, but they also considered her a bit of a drill sergeant, as she could be rather stern and demanding at times.

Ellen took her job very seriously. When she was hired at Middlebrook, the speech team had been floundering, but in three short years, she had developed her students into some of the best public speakers in the state. The college administrators were pleased with her performance and the prestige she had brought to Middlebrook by creating such a strong student group. Although she'd been assigned two graduate assistants, Ellen preferred to take charge of the day-to-day management of the team, and she often remarked on the challenge of keeping all these people moving in the same direction.

The laughter and conversation continued as the team members filed across the hall and took their places in the empty classroom. Sara Whitney plopped herself down at a table next to her friend Kevin Bates. As the other students took their places at tables, desks, and on the floor, she looked around the room and counted heads. Everyone was here tonight, which would probably make for a long meeting, and judging from the noise level, it would be a lively one. Most of the team members were wearing their "Middlebrook Speaking

Eagles Speech Team" T-shirts and chattering excitedly about all the events they'd won at the past weekend's competition. Sara felt a sense of belonging as she smiled at her fellow team members. When she came to Middlebrook as a freshman, she had wanted to get involved in an extracurricular activity and had looked into many clubs and organizations. The speech team had been the best fit, as it incorporated her love of public speaking with her major in communication.

Besides, the Speaking Eagles was the most prestigious organization on campus. Every fall, when tryouts were held to replace the few open positions on the team, students lined up to audition for Ellen and her graduate assistants. Only the very best had a chance of being selected to join a team that had a record of winning nearly every tournament they entered. The Speaking Eagles were the pride of Middlebrook and had been featured many times on the local news. The college had even used the team in a recruitment ad to show the public the high caliber of Middlebrook students. Members of the Speaking Eagles took great pride in being on the speech team and loved to wear their team shirts around campus.

The best thing about being on the team, though, was the close friendships Sara had developed in the two years since she'd joined. Because the Speaking Eagles spent so much time together—going on road trips to tournaments, staying in hotels, rehearsing for hours each week—they became like a second family. When Sara considered that she didn't know anyone when she first came to Middlebrook, she was very grateful to have this close and supportive group of friends to spend time with.

"Hey!" Ellen shouted over the din. "We have a lot to cover tonight, so listen up!" The noise level went down a notch. "Okay, first, I have the usual announcements. As usual, the Speaking Eagles had an awesome weekend, and we snatched up most of the awards!" The team members hooted and clapped, and Sara joined in. "Let's hear it for Barry Scovel, who took third in parliamentary debate and first in persuasion!"

More cheers and shouting followed, as Ellen read out the names of most of the members of the team and the individual awards they had won the previous weekend. Sara's mind started to drift. She never placed in as many categories as her teammates, even though it was her second year and she knew she was improving. Kevin had been a big help, listening to her rehearse and making suggestions for improvement. He was a senior and the star of the team, so Sara appreciated his help, even though he was demanding at times. She wanted to improve her skills and keep up with the highest achievers on the team. Most importantly, she didn't want to let her friends down, or disappoint Coach Redman.

" . . . and Sara Whitney took second in informative!" Sara's mind snapped back to the present as Ellen read out her name, and she blushed at the cheers and applause. A second-place finish in only one category put her near the bottom in terms of awards collected that past weekend; only Sam Kinnon, who didn't place at all, had done more poorly. At least she had the comfort of knowing that her individual win had contributed to the team's taking the overall tournament prize. Everyone knew that students who placed first, second, or third in each category were assigned points toward the team prize, and the team with the largest overall number of points were declared winners of the tournament. There was no bigger thrill than the moment your team was announced as the winner—everyone hugged, cheered, and even cried, and the excitement lasted all through the ceremony when the new trophies were added to the hallway case. In those moments, Sara felt an incredible bond with her teammates and knew she was a part of something very special.

Ellen continued by listing the two team trophies, and the excitement was deafening. "Okay, okay!" Ellen shouted, waving her arms. "Great job, guys, but that's done, it's behind us. We need to talk about this weekend's tournament at Lincoln University." Several students groaned. Lincoln was a much smaller school than Middlebrook and never performed very well in competition. Some of Sara's teammates liked to poke fun at the Lincoln students and call them losers, and to brag about how much better the Speaking Eagles were by comparison.

As if on cue, Kevin elbowed Sara in the side. "We're gonna dominate!" he smiled. "Piece of cake." Several other students echoed Kevin's thought, shouting "No problem!" and "It's ours!" along with some booing. Sara joined in, shouting "We'll take 'em!"

Ellen seemed pleased with her students' reaction. "That's right!" she grinned. "We're the top in the state, on our way to becoming the top in the nation, and don't you forget it!" The row of students behind Sara pumped their fists. "Those trophies are ours," Ellen continued. "I don't want a single one of you to let Lincoln, or anybody else, take *our* trophies! You got that? I've already cleared a place in the cabinet, and you guys had better fill it!"

Ellen always talked this way, and while it seemed to get Sara's teammates wound up, it made Sara a little bit nervous. Along with the fun and friendship of being on the team came a feeling of pressure to always do more and do better. Sara's grades had started to slip as she tried to balance the grueling schedule of constant rehearsing and weekly travel against her own classwork. She wanted to go to law school one day, so she had to keep her grades up. Quitting the speech team was not an option, though—the public speaking experience would help her get admitted into law school. Besides, she could never give up the feeling of pride she got from being a member of the team or the friendships she'd formed there. She knew that her classmates were impressed when they read her name in the student paper and passed by the trophy case in the classroom hall. She liked to wear her team shirt and to feel part of such an admired group on campus. Without the speech team, who was she? Just Sara Whitney, another communication major. Nobody special.

Sara knew that the next item on the meeting's agenda was the roll call, when each student would name the events he or she planned to take part in the following weekend. Ellen began to read the roster. "Kevin Bates!" she called, and Kevin sat up and smiled. "I'll do parliamentary debate, an informative, a persuasive, a dramatic interpretation, and a duo with Marty." Ellen nodded approvingly as she noted the events on the chalkboard. Kevin could always be counted on to enter a large number of events, and he usually won, or at least placed, in all of them. She turned back to the students and called the next name. "Chad Donaldson!"

Sara listened as each of her teammates rattled off the list of events in which they would compete. Nobody had entered fewer than three, except for Sam Kinnon, who drew snickers for naming only one event, his strongest: informative speaking. Some of the team members had already written Sam off as an underachiever, and few expected him to return next year. There were even rumors that Ellen wouldn't accept him on the team in the fall. Sara couldn't imagine being dropped from the team after enjoying the prestige of being a member. All of her friends were Speaking Eagles—or rather, the team made up her circle of friends—and she couldn't stand it if she wasn't able to see them every day and travel with them on weekends.

"Sara Whitney!" Ellen called. Sara was startled that her turn had come so quickly. "I'll do a dramatic reading and a persuasive," she said firmly, and Ellen noted the events on the board, then turned back with the chalk poised in her hand. "Yes?" Ellen said. "And what else?"

Sara blinked. "That's it."

"Oh, come on, Sara," D.J. Cooper laughed. "It's about time you tried duo, you'd be really good at it. You'd give us a great chance at the tournament trophy." The rest of the team picked up the idea and chanted, "Duo! Duo! Duo!"

"That's a great idea," Ellen said, and turned to write on the board. "I'll put you down for a duo with Max. He has one prepared already and just needs a partner." There was a general murmur of agreement: "Yeah, that'll work." "A duo with Max would be great." "A top score in a duo would really help us dominate."

Sara was speechless. She would never let her teammates down, but at the same time, she had a lot on her plate and there was no time in her schedule to rehearse a new event. She raised her hand. "Uh, Ellen? I really hadn't planned on doing three this weekend. Maybe . . ."

Ellen shrugged. "Max will help you. You'll be fine. Now, let's talk about the travel arrangements."

Sara sat with her head in her hands as Ellen talked about bus arrangements and hotel room reservations. They would be leaving on Thursday afternoon, right after Sara's final class of the week, and returning late on Sunday night, which meant that Sara would have the next two days to complete all of her homework for the coming week. Plus, there was the new event to rehearse with Max. She sighed. She had to attend the tournament; there were no two ways about that. She couldn't stand the thought of being left behind as her teammates boarded the bus without her. But at the same time, she couldn't imagine how she was going to finish writing two papers and get all of the reading for her courses done before Thursday.

Ellen clapped her hands to get everyone's attention. "Okay, everybody, that's it." She gestured to the chalkboard. "There's the lineup for this weekend. Now remember, you're all committed to this. It's time to dig in." She looked meaningfully at Sara. "Remember, we're the Speaking Eagles, best in the state!" The students cheered and clapped. "Now, I want all of you to go and rehearse, and those of you doing parliamentary debate need to show me your stuff before you leave tonight." The students prepared to disburse. "Oh, and Sara? Can I see you for a moment in my office?"

Sara's heart sank; was she in some kind of trouble? As her teammates returned to the bull pen and found places to sit on the stairs and in hallways, Sara dutifully followed Ellen to her office.

"Shut the door, Sara."

Sara obeyed and took a seat opposite Ellen's desk. She folded her hands in her lap and stared at Ellen, not knowing what to expect.

"Sara, how are things going for you this term?"

Sara shifted in her chair. "Just fine. I mean, it's hard to get all my homework done and keep my grades up while being on the team . . ." She bit her lip. "I don't want to let anybody down. I'm just . . ." Her head drooped. "I'm just tired."

Ellen hesitated. "I'm wondering if you might need a break from the team. If you're starting to burn out . . ."

"No!" Sara was startled at her own voice; she had shouted. "No," she repeated in a more controlled tone, "I don't want to quit. I understand the sacrifices I need to make."

"Sara, you're a very driven, ambitious young lady. I was a lot like you when I was a student." Ellen's expression softened. "You're not the first student to feel burned out from the demands of the speech team, and if it's taking a toll on your health and well-being, it might be time to let it go. Take the rest of the year off and audition again in the fall if you feel you can manage it."

"But—"

"You don't have to decide today. Go and rehearse with Max, and think it over in the next few days."

Sara realized she was being dismissed, so she got up and left the room. As she walked down the hallway in a daze, Max called out, "Hey, Sara, you ready to practice our duo?"

As she sat down on the stairs next to Max, he sensed her low mood. "Everything okay?" he asked. "Listen, Sara, I already have a script prepared, but if you'd rather do something else, I mean, if you have another piece in mind . . ."

"It's not that," Sara murmured. "It's nothing. I'm fine."

"What did Ellen have to say?"

"She thinks I'm getting burned out on . . . all this. She thinks maybe I need a break."

Max looked shocked. "A break, like, quit the team?"

"Yeah."

"Wow. What do you think?"

Sara hugged her knees. "I can't even imagine it. You guys are such a big part of my world. I love spending time with everybody here, I love the tournaments, I love being a part of the Speaking Eagles. On the other hand, I can't let my grades tank if I want to get into law school."

Max patted her arm. "I'm sure you'll make the right decision. We can go out later and talk about it some more. I'm just going to go get that script, okay?" As Max walked away, Sara buried her face in her hands. Despite Max's kind words, she couldn't see how things were going to get better. There were only so many hours in a day, and the stress of managing all of her obligations was getting intense. It was time to make some choices.

KEY TERMS

climate	identity
competition and collaboration	leadership
group norms	roles

DISCUSSION QUESTIONS

1. What norms can you identify in this group? How do you think these norms developed? How are these norms affecting Sara and other members?

2. How would you describe this group's climate? Is it mostly competitive or cooperative? How do you know?

3. What is the relationship between the group's climate and its norms?

4. How would you characterize Ellen's leadership style? What are the strengths and weaknesses of her leadership style?

5. How important is group identity to the members of this team? Why does group membership seem so important to Sara?

6. If you were Sara, what would you do? What are the important things for her to consider in her decision?

BUILDING INCLUSIVE SMALL GROUPS THROUGH INTEGRATED DANCE

Margaret M. Quinlan

A professional dance company for people with and without disabilities attempts to include a new dancer with disabilities into the company.

The Dancing Wheels Company & School[1] is the first professional modern dance company to integrate professional stand-up and sit-down (wheelchair) dancers in performances that seek to transform public understandings of disability. Located in Cleveland, Ohio, it collaborates with its parent organization, Professional Flair,[2] to bring educational outreach to audiences. Mary Verdi-Fletcher, Dancing Wheels' President and Founding Artistic Director and a pioneer in the field of integrated dance, started the company in 1980. For more than a quarter of a century, Dancing Wheels has performed, taught, and inspired children and adults of all abilities around the world. In the United States, the company annually produces more than one hundred performances, reaching a collective audience of 125,000 each year. In its fully accessible studio, Dancing Wheels provides community dance classes, summer dance workshops, theater arts camps, teacher training workshops, and specialized classes. Through these innovative programs that integrate arts and recreational activities with career opportunities and training, Dancing Wheels is committed to changing the apathy, negativity, and fear that surround the education, employment, and inclusion of persons with disabilities in the arts and broader communities. Through dance, the studio challenges cultural norms about the body and the institutional patterns and practices that fail to acknowledge and/or respond to different bodies. At any

---

[1]This case study is based on ethnographic data collected by Maggie Quinlan over an eighteen-month period while working with Dancing Wheels on her dissertation research. It is based on real events and people, but certain parts have been embellished for case study purposes.

[2]Professional Flair is a 501(c)(3) nonprofit organization that serves as the parent organization for Dancing Wheels and provides career opportunities and training in the arts for people with disabilities.

given time, the studio employs approximately eleven dancers (including both stand-up and sit-down dancers) who work with choreographers to challenge representations of a "normal" body as well as the opportunities and privileges that accompany it.[3] Dancing Wheels relies on aesthetic forms to foster more inclusive and diverse communities, including dance arenas. At Dancing Wheels, connection is created and expressed through dance. Integration and difference are central to Dancing Wheels' organizing practices and its ability to build a community inclusive of individuals who too often remain on the margins of civic life. Individuals with disabilities have historically been treated as objects of fear and pity and thought to be unwilling or unable to contribute to societal living.[4] For over twenty-nine years, Dancing Wheels has attempted to combat negative perceptions of individuals with disabilities by showing that they can be contributing members of society.

MARK ARRIVES AT THE STUDIO

Mark Daurelio wheels into the studio for the first time. His noticeably chiseled arms and athletic frame grab the other dancers' attention. Mark's wheelchair is better suited for wheelchair basketball than integrated dance, as his basketball chair noticeably has a fifth wheel on the back and a bumper on the front so toes do not get crushed. Also, the wheels on his basketball chair are set at 12-degree angles for the stability needed in wheelchair basketball.

"You finally decided to join us," says Mary Verdi-Fletcher. Mary had been trying to recruit him for several years after they met at a basketball tournament. "Well, the best way to give you an idea of how the company works is to throw you into the mix," explains Mary. "He's cute," mumble two stand-up dancers, Sara and Kristen. They both giggle. "Okay, Mark, tell me what you can do in your chair," says Mary. "Well, in wheelchair basketball, I'm able to do wheelies and I am in pretty good shape, so I'm able to move relatively fast. My apartment building is not very accessible, so I'm able to go up and down several flights of stairs," says Mark.

"Nice. We are looking to start choreographing new and exciting, fast pieces of repertory. It's what audiences want to see and Mark Tomasic, a stand-up dancer and choreographer, has just choreographed *A Wing/A Prayer,* an all-wheeler piece. We'd like to see you in it as soon as possible," notes Mary. "Just remember I haven't danced before," Mark nervously remarks. "We will train you with everything you need to know," explains Mac, a stand-up dancer, who came to Cleveland to dance with the company from Viet Nam.

"We're going to start with a warm-up and teach you some of our basic movements. Most of the movements we do are what we call in integrated dance, translation, where we translate movement from a stand-up to a sit-down dancer. Mac will show you the movement

---

[3]Dancing Wheels. (2010). Retrieved April 30, 2010 from http://www.dancingwheels.org/

[4]R. Funk, "Disability Rights: From Caste to Class in the Context of Civil Rights," in *Images of the Disabled, Disabling Images,* ed. A. Gartner and T. Joe, 7–30 (New York: Praeger, 1987).

that he'll be doing, and then we'll creatively figure out a way to translate it to you. Jenny, a sit-down dancer who has been with the company the longest, will also be demonstrating how she is able to translate movement for her body," Mary says.

"I'm not really sure if dance is my thing. So go easy on me," Mark says. "First thing we will need to do is have you switch out of your basketball chair into one that is better suited for dance. We have extra chairs in the studio, but if you decide to work with us, we'll work on fundraising to get you your own chair for when you perform," said Mary. Mark transfers chairs and straps in his feet as Mary explains, "The one thing you'll need to remember is that in modern dance, you are telling a story with your body. And you'll need to get emotion out through your face and body."

Stand-up dancer Mac calls out, "I need everyone to sit down on the ground or in your chair. Cross your right leg under your left leg and point your left leg. Fold your body over the tops of your legs, and then windmill both arms up with your right arm leading. Have your left arm follow. With your right arm behind your body/chair, place your right arm back on the floor with your left arm up in the air. For the wheelers, you will want to touch your arm to the floor so that your feet are up in the air and you are doing a wheelie." Mark watches Jenny go through the motions and then copies her movements. He windmills his right arm to the floor behind his chair and into a wheelie. He struggles to touch the ground and once he does, his right arm is shaking, and he falls and slides out of the back of the chair. With a red and embarrassed face, Mark unstraps his feet from his wheelchair and gets back into his chair as Mary comfortably says, "Falling is part of dancing, it's how we learn about what our body can do." Mark replies, "I guess I should have mentioned that because of where I broke my back in the motocross accident, I'm paralyzed from the belly button down, a T-10 spinal cord injury, and don't have the trunk strength that others may have."

"Yeah, well, Mary and I both were born with spina bifida,[5] so we may have more trunk strength, but I bet you're fast on your wheels and can turn quickly. Let's see how we can use your upper body strength while dancing. Remember, all chairs move a little differently, just like all legs are not able to do the same movements," says Jenny. She continues, "Dancing in a chair is not as easy as it looks. I started at Dancing Wheels when I was four. I'm trying to let audiences know that not all dancers need to move their legs."

CELEBRATING DIFFERENCE IN SMALL GROUP COMMUNICATION

"Well, I guess I'm not sure what you mean by integration," says Mark. Mark Tomasic, a stand-up dancer and choreographer with the company, says, "For me, integration is the combining of different types of people or parts in harmony. Integrated dance, then, is the

---

[5]Spina bifida is a developmental birth defect caused by the incomplete closure of the embryonic neural tube. Some vertebrae overlying the spinal cord are not fully formed and remain unfused and open. If the opening is large enough, this allows a portion of the spinal cord to stick out through the opening in the bones. There may or may not be a fluid-filled sac surrounding the spinal cord.

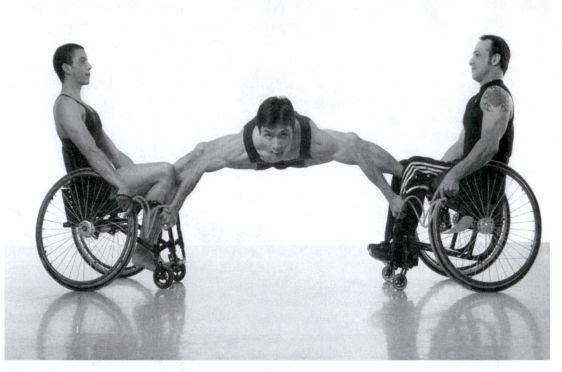

FIGURE 1—*Mark Daurelio (right), Hoang Dang (Mac) (middle), Isaah Henderson (left). Courtesy of Dale Dong.*

rhythmic movement to music of different types of people resulting in a whole." Mary continues, "We see difference as an opportunity for us to think of creative movements and find different ways of bringing bodies together. Our philosophy is that we want to focus on individuals' abilities rather than their (dis)abilities." Sara, a stand-up dancer, adds, "Yeah, at Dancing Wheels difference or diversity isn't seen as a problem that needs to be fixed and made 'normal' again. However, at Dancing Wheels, we reconceptualize problem solving as a way for choreographers and dancers to think outside the box of movement possibilities and choices. Just when we think there are no more movement possibilities, we come along and meet a new dancer who has different abilities that we try to capitalize on and integrate it into the dance."

"Don't get me wrong, Mark, as artistic director I do make the final decisions in the company, but I do work with dancers to find the essence of strength to make the best dance production possible. I do rely on the dancers and the choreographers to think of new movement possibilities. Dancers don't always agree with my decisions, but with the economy being the way it is, we need to keep audiences coming back . . ." Kristen, a stand-up dancer, interrupts. "Since in dance we are dependent on trusting our partners to do and be where they need to be, I need to know that I can trust my partner to catch me when I am coming out of a lift."

"If member of our company aren't getting along or fighting, we need to address these issues or someone could get seriously hurt," says Sara, a stand-up. Mary adds, "We actually rely on moments where dancers are frustrated to help us be creative when we are out of ideas about how to bring a dance together. When we have eleven dancers and they are all sweating, dealing with injuries, there are bound to be tears. I would like to start having morning meetings with the dancers, where we start talking about some of the issues dancers are facing. But it is difficult since dancers are coming in and out of the studio all day, and it is difficult to find a time that we are all here together."

"Sometimes, I get really frustrated when I feel like a rolling prop. Some choreographers come in here and don't know what to do with us sit-down dancers. It is like we are placed in the dance as an afterthought," says Jenny. "When I am bored or don't feel like my dancing abilities are used, I threaten to quit. I have quit a few times . . ." Jenny sighs. "But I keep coming back because there are not many career options for people with disabilities and these people are like my family. I mean, Mary has practically raised me."

"I've learned a lot about this company from one fall, and I have not even made it past the warm-up. Thanks for your patience with me. I'd like to give this dancing gig a shot. I need to figure out how to work with my wheelchair basketball schedule," says Mark.

KEY TERMS

communication climate	leadership competencies
cohesiveness	new member socialization
diversity	relational communication
inclusion	trust

DISCUSSION QUESTIONS

1. How would you describe the communication climate of this group? What examples of supportive relational communication do you see in this group?

2. In what ways are these group members interdependent?

3. What advantages are there to this company to developing cohesiveness? What are some of the material and physical consequences if members do not develop cohesiveness? When could cohesiveness create problems for this group?

4. Why is disability an issue of diversity that is often overlooked in small group communication? How would you describe Dancing Wheels' approach to including individuals with and without disabilities in dance?

5. Have you ever been involved in a group or a team where you had to include people of all different abilities? If so, what did you do? Or what would you have done differently?

6. How does the company deal with procedural, relational and task competencies in leadership? Do you have any suggestions for how they can operate more effectively?

GROUP SOCIALIZATION

The Newcomer Experience in a Community Choir

Michael W. Kramer

A new member deals with doubts and uncertainty during the process of joining a community choir.

Ralph was excited about attending his first rehearsal of the Midwest Community Choir (MCC). After singing in high school and university choirs, he found singing in his church choir less than challenging. He hoped joining MCC would provide an opportunity to sing challenging music, perform for large audiences, and meet new people in the community.

Ralph found out about MCC through a church choir friend, Roselyn, who was a member of MCC off and on. Currently she was taking a break from it because her son was in soccer, and it was just too much effort to coordinate their schedules. Roselyn emphasized to Ralph that one nice thing about MCC was that "You can come and go according to your schedule and no one seems to mind." Since she wouldn't be there, Ralph wasn't sure he would know anyone.

Ralph double-checked the time and location on MCC's website and learned more about the group. It said that there was an audition, but that anyone could come to a rehearsal. This was the first rehearsal of the fall season after their summer break, and so this seemed like a good time to join.

Ralph entered the lobby of the local high school where MCC rehearsed with a bit of anxiety, unsure of what to expect. There were groups of people standing around talking and a long line at what looked like a registration table. Ralph was concerned he would be late by the time he made it through the line, but it moved fairly quickly.

Near the front of the line Mark, the group's director, recognized Ralph as a newcomer and said, "You're new, right?" As Ralph nodded, Mark continued, "Welcome to MCC. I think you'll enjoy the people and the singing. Sarah can help you get registered."

With that he directed Ralph to Sarah, the woman at the far end of the table. Sarah was used to handling the newcomers. She asked him his name and asked him to fill out an information form while she made him a name tag. As she handed it to him she said, "You'll get your permanent name tag next week. Now, do you want to buy or borrow the music?"

Since Ralph had no idea what the cost might be, he mumbled, "Borrow, I guess," and she handed him several pieces of music and a CD. "What's this?" he asked.

"It's a CD of the music we're doing for the first two concerts so that you can listen to it at home to practice." Ralph was a surprised that he was expected to practice the music at home. When he asked about the audition, Sarah just said, "Don't worry about that. Just go in and find a seat. You wrote that you're a tenor. Tenors sit on the right side of the aisle." As he headed into the room, she wondered whether he would be a one-timer who never returned after the first rehearsal or become a regular.

When Ralph entered the rehearsal room, he realized that there were two kinds of name tags—temporary ones like his and permanent ones. This distinguished newcomers from old-timers, but at least it made it easier to learn people's names.

When he looked at the section where the tenors were supposed to sit he was surprised that there was a mixture of men and women. He asked a man, "Is this the tenor section?"

The man, whose temporary tag said Bob, said, "I think so, but it's just my first time. I guess some of the women sing tenor."

When Rachel, who was sitting in the row behind them, heard this comment, she recognized that they must be newcomers and leaned over and said, "Hi, I'm Rachel, and yes, there are a lot of women who sing tenor in this choir. It's just one of the things we do differently here." By the time Ralph and Bob introduced themselves, the director, Mark, took his place at the front of the room and made a brief opening announcement.

"Welcome to the fall season of Midwest Community Choir. It's so exciting to have all of you here, the new faces and the returning ones. We have a lot to do this evening and I'll have some announcements at the break, but we're here to sing and so let's get started! Everybody stand for warm-ups." With that he sang a run of notes for warm-ups, and everyone stood and sang along as they worked their way first up higher and higher and then back down. Old-timers straggled in during the warm-ups, and there were probably 100 people present by the time they finished.

Then Mark told everyone to sit and take out Verdi's *Triumphal March,* one of the pieces everyone received at registration. Ralph was surprised that it was in Italian. He had never sung in any language besides English or Latin., He found it extremely difficult to sing along trying to watch the notes and figure out the words at the same time.

Mark recognized that new members had never sung this particular piece and often had trouble singing in a foreign language. At one of the stopping points, he said, "I know that some of you old-timers know this from singing it last year, and that those of you who are new may feel kind of lost. Don't worry about it. You'll catch on. I don't expect you to get it all tonight." Mark did stop a couple times to tell people how to correctly pronounce phrases, but Ralph found that he forgot the correct pronunciation by the time it came up again.

Once when only the altos and sopranos were singing, Ralph asked Bob if he was lost. He was relieved when Bob said, "Yeah, I'm lost. It's all Greek to me." The group spent most of the first hour on this piece with Ralph and Bob only feeling slightly better by the end of that time. They guessed that Mark went through it quickly because so many people knew most of it.

Fortunately, when Mark told them to turn to the second piece, it was very familiar to Ralph. He had sung this particular version of "The Battle Hymn of the Republic" back in high school and practically knew it from memory. He was a little disappointed that they only sang through it once, corrected one spot, and then it was time for the break. Mark said to be back in ten minutes.

During the break, the old-timers, with their permanent name tags, greeted each other like old friends. Most of them didn't feel like making an effort to talk to newcomers. They took a wait-and-see attitude because they knew that some of them would quit after one or two rehearsals. Feeling a bit excluded as a result, Ralph and Bob talked to each other and found out that they both joined at the encouragement of friends, but neither knew anyone there that evening. They briefly discussed their work and families. They didn't have a lot in common, other than that they enjoyed singing. Just before the break ended, an old-timer, Carol, introduced herself to them and welcomed them to the tenor section. She re-inforced that if they were feeling a little lost that was okay. She said, "I felt that way at first, but now I don't worry about it because it always comes together for the concert." Before they could say much more, Mark tapped the music stand to get everyone's attention and began making announcements.

Mark's announcements included procedures for signing in for attendance and the date for their first concert in just four weeks. He told everyone not to worry because they were doing just four short pieces. Two were easy pieces and one was familiar to most of them from last year. The fourth was a selection from Faure's *Requiem,* the major work for their second concert in two months. They would spend the first half of rehearsals on those four pieces, but the second half on the rest of the *Requiem.* Mark knew that the newcomers were probably feeling lost, but he felt like he needed to hurry through the announcements because there was so much music to learn, and so he asked that all newcomers to stay after rehearsal for a while so that he could talk to them separately. With that, he had everyone take out the *Requiem* and turn to the "Sanctus." It was in Latin.

Because no one knew this piece, Mark went considerably slower, but still moved pretty quickly through it. When someone raised a hand to ask him a question, he said, "No ques-tions right now, because we'll be working on this for several weeks. And remember, you all received the CD with the music. You can listen to it and learn on your own between re-hearsals." After that, no one raised their hands as they worked on three different parts of the *Requiem.* Ralph often felt lost, but not as much as on the Italian piece. It helped that he was able to hear some of the tenors around him. He also figured out to listen to the women who were singing tenor in addition to men.

About two hours after they started, Mark thanked everyone and reminded the newcomers to stay and come together in the middle of the room for a brief orientation meeting. When they gathered, it seemed that like they made up about one-fourth of the choir.

Because he had a number of conversations with various old-timers first, Mark was a little slow getting to the newcomer group. As he thought about what to say, he wanted to be sure to encourage the newcomers to return, and so he began with, "Thank you all for coming. New members are the life blood of this choir. It is through you that the group stays vibrant and energized. It invigorates me as the director to see all of you new people." Ralph felt pretty good about those comments; it was nice to be appreciated.

Next Mark told the newcomers, "I know the web page said, and some of you may have heard, that there is an audition, but there really isn't one. I just put that up so that people who come are serious about singing. You are all welcome as long as you feel comfortable." Everyone in the newcomer group seemed relieved by that.

Next, in an effort to relieve some anxieties that he knew the newcomers felt at their first rehearsal, Mark reiterated his early announcement. "I know many of you may have felt rushed and lost tonight. That is completely normal. But I am confident that if you stick with it, you will all catch up by the first concert, even though it is in just four weeks. There's a special rehearsal that Friday evening to prepare. And remember, you can listen to the CD to learn what you don't get at rehearsal. There simply is not enough time to go over everything in detail for each of the four sections during rehearsal, and so I rely on you learning some of it on your own."

This was a new idea for Ralph. In all his previous choir experiences, he had never had to practice outside of rehearsal. He generally learned the music faster than others, but after this first rehearsal, he thought that he might need to practice outside rehearsal. Finding time for that was a bit of a concern for him, but he could probably manage.

Then Mark briefly explained a number of other things. "Concert dress is tuxes for men and black dresses for women. If any of you men need a tux, you can rent one or next week, Alex, the owner of Tuxedo Junction, will be here to help fit you. And Alex will give you a big discount." Ralph hadn't realized he would have to own a tux to sing in MCC and from a quick glance, he could tell that Bob hadn't expected it either.

Mark knew that he needed to clarify some of the financial aspects of the group. He always hated making these announcements, but the reality of conducting a nonprofit choir was that you were always asking for money. He continued, "You all are welcome to use the music for free as long as you return it, or you can buy it. The *Requiem* is $20, but the other pieces are not for sale. Now the last thing that I need to tell you is that ticket sales simply do not cover our costs. We rely on donations from the audience and from the members. We recommend that members donate $40 per concert to help make ends meet. Now I know that is not possible for some of you, and for others it will be no problem. Some of you will give more and some less. It is completely voluntary, and I want you to know that I would rather have a heartfelt donation of whatever amount than a begrudging larger one. But of course, no donation is too large." Everyone laughed at that. He continued, "The most important thing is that you be part of the group and sing with your hearts."

After that, Mark made two quick announcements. "You will each receive one free ticket to each concert to give to your spouse, partner, significant other, or just some random person on the street." Again everyone laughed. He finished with, "And please, if you have any questions, e-mail me. My e-mail is on the website. See you next week."

Most of the old-timers were already cleared out by the end of the newcomer orientation. As Ralph left, the only person who said good-bye was Bob, but he wasn't sure anyone else would have said anything anyway. The old-timers were a bit cliquish, at least on this first night.

As he drove home, Ralph considered quitting after just one week. He was a little concerned about having to buy a tux and make a "voluntary" donation to the group, but his biggest concern was that he didn't think he could be ready for the first concert even if he worked on the music outside of rehearsal time. He knew that there was no way he would feel confident singing the *March* in Italian and the "Sanctus" in Latin in just four weeks. Then he remembered what Roselyn said about it being okay to drop in and out of MCC. He decided to attend all of the regular rehearsals and simply skip the first concert. With such a big group, he doubted that anyone would miss him at the concert anyway. He felt like he could be ready for the second concert since there was more time until it. He definitely wanted to be in the third concert, Handel's *Messiah*. That was the real reason he had joined the group. He had always wanted to do that piece with a large group.

The next three rehearsals went pretty much as Ralph expected. He received his permanent name tag. He still did not feel confident singing the piece in Italian and only slightly better with the Latin. So he simply skipped the special rehearsal and the first concert. He felt a little out of it when Mark discussed how well the concert had gone at the next rehearsal, but otherwise it didn't seem to matter that he had missed it. The only person who asked about his absence was Bob, who admitted that he had to fake the Italian piece, and so he stood in the back where no one could see him, and that worked out okay.

By the time of the second concert Ralph felt a little more like a part of the group. He knew quite a few more people by name, mostly the tenors who sat near him. They didn't have assigned seats, but people tended to sit in about the same places anyway, and so he talked to the same people most weeks, including Bob, Rachel, and Carol. He met a couple people from other sections who shared his interest in theater when he overheard them talking about a community theater group and introduced himself to them and joined in their conversation. After that, he talked to them almost every week either before rehearsal or during the break. They talked about seeing a show together sometime soon.

More importantly, as the concert approached, Ralph felt like he knew the music. He had listened to the CD a little—mostly in the car on the way to work. At home, he used his piano to learn a couple spots that were difficult. He managed to find a tux at a department store that cost a lot less than the so-called discount he was going to receive at Tuxedo Junction. He still hadn't made a donation to the group, but it hadn't been mentioned again and so he wasn't feeling pressured at this time.

The extra two rehearsals the week of the concert went well and singing the music three times in one week before the concert really helped to build everyone's confidence. Because he was proud of what the group was accomplishing, Ralph gave his free ticket to Roselyn and invited a number of other friends to the concert. He was pleased when he spotted them in the audience as he was waiting to sing. It turned out to be a fun evening, first performing and then talking to them afterward. As he drove home after the concert, he looked forward to working on Handel's *Messiah* next, and since he felt more confident about being a member of the group, he thought he could invite more people to see the next performance, and maybe he would get to go see a theater production with his new friends soon.

KEY TERMS

group climate	task and relational communication
group development	norms
group membership	socialization
roles	

DISCUSSION QUESTIONS

1. What experiences and communication processes led people to join MCC? Be sure to consider both what led Ralph and Bob to seek out MCC and MCC's efforts to recruit new members.

2. What are some of the important group norms of MCC that a newcomer must learn? What were some of the significant surprises or unmet expectations that Ralph experienced when he joined MCC?

3. How did the communication and attitudes of the director and old-timers of the group affect Ralph's experiences as a newcomer?

4. How are the experiences of joining a group as a voluntary member similar or different to joining a group as an employee? What would have been different if the group were part of Ralph's job expectations?

5. How can events of this case help other volunteer organizations or community groups?

¡La lucha y conducción grupal!

A Workshop for Youth Members of a Nicaraguan Fair Trade Coffee Cooperative[1]

Leah M. Sprain

Nicaraguan youth attend a capacity-building workshop hosted by a local fair trade coffee cooperative.

NICARICA[2] is a fair trade coffee cooperative in northern Nicaragua. NICARICA has six hundred fifty members (adults and youth) who belong to fifteen member cooperatives. Members join the cooperatives in order to gain leverage in the international market. Small farmers bind together to sell their high-quality coffee to buyers in Europe and the United States for higher prices than individual farmers could secure on their own. Cooperatives are economic organizations, but many cooperatives also aim to improve the lives of members. Often this includes offering training and social services to members.

Recently, the cooperative invited twenty-eight youth members of NICARICA to attend a *taller*, a capacity-building workshop, on methods of group leadership. This workshop was designed to train youth on different methods of running and setting up meetings. Over the course of three days, youth engaged in activities and lessons about what it takes to organize events and lead groups in their communities. Since most of the teens were already leaders of youth groups in their cooperatives, the workshop had the practical goal of helping youth to organize at least one meeting or event in the next few months. Events

---

[1] This case study is based on a workshop the author observed during field research at a coffee cooperative in Nicaragua. This case study is based on real events, but the names of participants have been changed and some of the dialogue has been adapted for the case study. This case study is informed by real events, but it should not be read as a transcript of real comments. As much as possible, the cultural details have not been changed or embellished.

[2] NICARICA is my name for an organization of coffee farmers in northern Nicaragua. NICARICA appears in all caps to follow the local style of using acronyms as cooperative names. NICARICA, however, is not an acronym. Instead, it is a slight play on words. *Nica* is slang for Nicaraguan. *Rica* means both rich (in money) and delicious (like the coffee they produce).

could include educational workshops about topics such as organic fertilizer, literacy, or finances, fun activities (community theater or music workshops), or meetings to plan future activities. More broadly, the workshop helped build the capacity of youth to lead their local cooperatives.

The workshop on group leadership was scheduled to begin at 7:30 a.m. At 7:30 a.m., three youth were quietly sitting in chairs set up in rows facing a table and whiteboard in the front of the room. As the minutes passed, more youth came in and sat down. Some teens knew each other and sat in clusters, catching up and gossiping about other goings on in their communities. Graysen and Maria Delia had been lucky enough to attend a course on roasting coffee three months prior. They enjoyed chatting, sharing stories. Other teens didn't know anyone and sat quietly in their seats. This was Pablo's first visit to the main office. He wasn't even sure exactly why he was there, but his father had insisted he come to make the most of this opportunity.

At 8:15 a.m., Luisa, who worked for the cooperative, came in and asked to have the chairs rearranged into a large circle with thirty chairs. A sign-in sheet was passed around to get the names of all the participants.

The workshop facilitator, Jose, arrived at 8:35 a.m. He immediately began with an activity in which everyone needed to get the names of sixteen different people in a chart that looked like a bingo board. No one could sit down until his or her sheet was full of names. The room was frenzied as everyone tried to fill in the sheets. Maria Delia, who knew lots of other people, began to fill in the boxes on her sheet with names simply by looking around. Others, like Pablo, had to ask people for their names. As people began to sit down with completed squares, others frantically tried to fill in their squares so they too could sit down. Once everyone had full squares, Jose had people introduce themselves, sharing their name, a positive personal characteristic about themselves, and what they hoped to get out of the workshop. When someone introduced him- or herself, everyone who had that person on their bingo board marked off that square. When someone got four squares in a row, he or she got a prize: a packet of cookies. The movement back and forth between introductions and shouting out "Bingo!" kept everyone engaged.

After introductions, the facilitator wrote *dinámica* (dynamic) on the whiteboard. Before anyone could take notes, Jose insisted, "Put your notebooks away. Too often at workshops people spend all of their time taking notes and writing things down. Not today. Put away your notebooks. I'll give you a full book of notes for you to read at home, but when we are together, we are going to be active. We are going to learn by doing, and in doing activities you will discover what it means to be good group leaders. As the leader of this workshop, I will guide you through activities. But I also need you. I need you to share your experiences and perspectives. Together we will learn from each other."

Motioning back to the board, Jose asked participants for words that relate when he talked about something being dynamic. Volunteers were given whiteboard markers to write their words. Movement. Energy. Fun. Excitement. Jose repeated the activity with *técnica* (technique or skills) and *juego* (play or game), ensuring that everyone in the workshop wrote at least one word on the whiteboard.

When this brainstorming was complete, the facilitator noted that a lot of the words could fit into all the categories in various ways. But these words were not the same. "Dynamics are about the interaction of the group. Nothing more or nothing less. Play is about socialization, everything that we learn about life through interacting with each other. In the middle is the technical, the skills that we must learn to lead and act in groups." These three words provide the backbone of the session, insisted Jose.

Jose moved swiftly into the next activity where all the participants were told to get into order by their birthdates. After they successfully got in order by day of the month, Jose pointed to a large log and said to do it again by birth month—but this time everyone must start standing on top of the log and reorder without stepping off the log. People carefully negotiated around each other. When someone stepped off, everyone had to start over. Moving around, David wanted to check in with Maria Jesus before touching her at all. Maria Jesus just smiled and accepted his offer of support. With some nervous laughter, concentration, and only a few missteps, the group rearranged itself in the new order.

Having achieved the goal, everyone sat back down in seats arranged in the circle, where Jose asked a series of processing questions. "How did you feel?" probed Jose.

"Well, uncomfortable at first," replied David.

"Why?" pushed Jose.

"We were standing so close to each other," said David. "I'm not used to having to be so close and rely on other people to achieve a task. I wasn't sure about other people; I didn't know whether they would be able to keep on top of the log without my help."

"What about the girls?"

"I guess I wanted to help them," continued David. "I wasn't sure if they would be comfortable having me touch them, but I wanted to help support them so we could all stay on the log."

"But you touched the girls to help them out?" asked Jose.

"Yeah, I figured that was part of it. I figured helping each other was part of the game."

"But not all of the guys helped all the girls," mused Jose. "Some of the guys kept their hands to themselves. And more than that, few of the guys touched other guys. Why do you think that was?"

Nervous laughter echoed in the room, but none of the youth responded to Jose's question. He let it hang in the air for an extended moment. Seconds passed as teens thought about why they did and did not touch each other.

Then, swiftly, Jose transitioned to another activity. The group moved from passing objects around the circle to taking off extra clothing items and jewelry to spell out words to playing tag. Each of these games lasted long enough to actually play them. Participants were clearly having fun, laughing and smiling. At the end of each activity, Jose asked a few questions to process the activity. He asked about how it felt to finish the activity first, how it felt to lose the game of tag, how it felt to be the one to drop the passed object.

Pablo started to relax a bit. He didn't need to worry about not knowing anyone. Each activity made it easy to join in, meeting new people as he went. Even the processing questions were interactive, although a few of them were tough questions that he didn't really have answers to. Pablo was happy when he didn't get called on. But he enjoyed participating in the games.

Jose seemed to know just what to do to keep everyone engaged in the activities and discussions. He seemed always in control and yet ready to bend, depending on the comments and perspectives of the teen participants.

In between activities, Jose addressed the group. "So what is this about: dynamics, skills, or games?"

"Games," replied Margarita.

"Excellent," replied Jose. "These are all games. They are play. In some of these cases, play is a way to learn skills, to learn technical information. But some of these are just games, nothing more, nothing less. Are these games dialogue?"

"Yes!" shouted Javier.

"No!" shouted Jose in response. "No. Dialogue is more than just play. Dialogue is more than just skills. Dialogue is more than just fun. Dialogue is a way of engaging and meeting each other, of learning with each other, of engaging each other so that we really see and relate. What is the purpose of games?"

"To laugh?" suggested Pablo.

"Yes, to laugh. It is so great to laugh. Sometimes play is simply about making people come together to relate and laugh. Sometimes it is more. Sometimes games can be a way of experiencing particular concepts and ideas; play can be a way of engaging rather than just sitting in a circle listening to someone lecture. But sometimes play alone is not enough. Sometimes we need to get to dialogue. Yes?"

"Yes," echoed the youth.

During these interactions, Jose captured the attention of the room. The energy from the activities—the energy of running, moving, scheming, and plotting—carried into the discussions. Youth were eager to participate, their eyes fixed on Jose and their mouths generally open to shout out an answer or interjection.

Jose introduced the last activity before lunch, an activity called problem trees. "Draw a tree. Your tree should represent a problem. Figure out a big name for your problem. And then you need to draw it. The leaves are social, the trunk organizational, and the roots political or economic. That is, when you draw the leaves offer all of the different social aspects of the problem, as many as you can think of. The trunk is made up of the ways that the organization supports or reflects your problem. And finally, the roots represent the social and economic factors that feed and structure your problem. So you will draw a tree, but that tree will be made up of all of these different factors through words on your drawing." Jose divided the youth into four groups of seven.

One of the groups selected **communication** as their problem. Javier, Pablo, Graysen, Tito, Eslin, Angelita, and Adayari talked about how one of the biggest problems in the cooperative was the lack of communication.

"What do you think is really the problem with communication? What do we mean by a communication problem?" asked Javier.

"Sometimes there is a refusal to listen, to accept other points of view," noted Angelita.

"Yeah, we tell people to shut up or just walk away, instead of really listening," added Adayari.

Pablo acknowledged, "Sometimes I think that there is a fear of sharing an opinion or telling a point of view."

"Distrust," interjected Eslin.

"Yeah, distrust. Sometimes I think that we don't really rely on each other," said Angelita.

"Where do we find distrust in our cooperatives?" asked Javier.

"Well, sometimes distrust means that we don't feel comfortable confiding in other people about important topics," said Eslin. "I mean, sometimes we don't say the things that we should."

"Sometimes distrust means something a bit different," said Tito. "Distrust means that we don't feel comfortable talking, don't feel comfortable sharing our ideas or our points of view."

"If distrust is the problem," probed Jose, who happened to be listening to the group discussion, "then how do we solve it?"

"Capacity-building," said Eslin. "Perhaps we need a workshop on communication or human relations."

Angelita added, "Respect. I think we need respect for other points of view."

"Yeah, respect," said Adayari. "Or more conversation."

"Just like this workshop," said Pablo. "I think the things that we are doing right now are really good. I think that some of this could be used to change the communication problem."

"Sometimes we need more delineation of responsibility. If it isn't clear whose job it is, things can be more difficult," added Tito.

"What do you mean?" probed Javier.

"Well, like the manager," continued Tito. "I mean, everyone knows that she does a good job. But sometimes I think that she doesn't really communicate with everyone. We don't always know what is going on. We rely on her to make decisions. This is part of our communication problem. We don't talk to each other enough, but we also don't really trust each other with important issues and decisions. Too often we have to rely on someone else."

After completing their problem trees, all the teens headed to lunch at a nearby restaurant. Over plates of chicken, rice, and beans, the youth shared stories and laughed. With some prompting by cooperative workers, they walked back to the cooperative office to continue the afternoon session of the workshop.

Jose started the afternoon by getting the group to generate a list of various words for the person leading a group. Facilitator. Instructor. Capacity-builder. Extension agent. Leader. Coordinator. Promotor. Guide. Actor. Communicator. Boss. Animator. Monitor. Director. Teacher. "All of these words are really saying *educator*," said Jose.

He transitioned to discussing four different types of leaders: authoritarian, paternal, laissez-faire, and democratic. Youth were split into groups; each group needed to figure out ways to act out each leadership style in a skit. The groups talked through the advantages and disadvantages of each style.

"Authoritarian leaders tell people what to do," started Eslin.

"They are controlling," added Maria Delia.

"They get things done, though," noted Angelita. "An authoritarian style can ensure that decisions are made and things are clear."

The group fell into silence for a few moments. "Let's see," mused Maria Delia. "Paternal leaders care about the group members as though they were family members—what a loving way to lead a group."

"But sometimes paternal leaders are still critical of group members just like authoritarian leaders," said Angelita. "This can lead to hurt feelings just the same."

Tito insisted, "A laissez-faire style is too loose. When anything goes, nothing ever gets done. I think it is really like no leadership at all."

"Really?" asked Maria Delia. "Because I think that a laissez-faire style respects participants in a group. It gives them the freedom to act and lead. That respects people in the group. It gives room for creativity, allowing participants to make things happen that would be impossible with a dictator in charge."

Angelita transitioned to the last type of leadership. "Democratic leadership also gives people freedom to provide input to the group and influence decisions. But at the same time, democratic leaders provide some structure for the group. Not just anything goes."

"Democratic leaders make sure that each opinion is considered before moving on to make a decision," noted Eslin.

The group went on to plan their skits, exaggerating the good and bad characteristics of each type of leader in their dramatic presentations.

In the last discussion of the day, Jose talked about the importance of the meanings of non-verbal communication. Group leaders must understand the different ways that people can interpret nonverbal codes. For example, there are multiple types of silence. A group leader must know when to let the group be silent and when to interrupt. "There are clear and dark silences. Sometimes silences are full of thinking that has been prompted by a particular question. These silences can be really important for a group. Other times silences just mean that people don't know what to say.

"So, how can a leader know which silence is which?" asked Jose. His question was met with silence. "No one?" After waiting five seconds and scanning the room with his eyes looking for someone willing to speak, Jose continued, "Okay, sometimes you need to learn body language and how to read people's positions. For example, when someone is standing with their arms crossed, leaning against the wall, what does their body language say?"

"Relaxed. They look really cool, comfortable, really chill," answered Pablo.

"No," countered Jose. "They are closed off. Disconnected from the group. They are cutting themselves off by closing their arms, showing that they aren't interested in learning new things."

The day ended with a short discussion of things that the teens appreciated and liked about the day's workshop.

"It was so interactive. It was dynamic. The entire thing was dynamic," Graysen said.

"There were no notes," added Maria Delia. "I really liked that we put down our notebooks and were active instead of just sitting there in rows."

Tito mused, "Like other people have said, this workshop felt really different. We were active and involved. I felt like we were engaged in learning new things, doing them instead of just studying them."

"At first, I wasn't really sure why I was here and didn't know anyone," admitted Pablo. "But all of the games made it really easy to meet people. I feel like I've been included, brought into the group. Plus I've learned a few things."

EPILOGUE

After a full day leading the workshop, Jose headed upstairs to lead another meeting for a group of cooperative employees. On the way up the stairs, he leaned over to me, a researcher studying the cooperative, and asked what I thought of the workshop. I replied that I found it really interesting. I was at the cooperative to study communication, culture, and meetings. Many of the activities and discussions during the workshop touched on these themes. I found it fascinating. Plus, I had led similar activities and conversations in the United States, both in communication classrooms and in community groups. I was intrigued by the similarities and differences between this NICARICA workshop and my own experiences teaching and studying group communication.

Jose paused and looked directly at me. "In order to understand today's workshop, you need to understand that it comes from a Latin American context. It is about la lucha [the struggle] and the desire to create dialogue."

"What do you mean by dialogue?" I asked.

"Dialogue means transformation. It means creating the conditions for change, talking into order to transform. Dialogue is the means of struggling for transformation. In order to understand, you must understand Latin America. This workshop is about the Latin American struggle to overcome. This workshop isn't just about leadership or groups or meetings. It is about la *lucha*. I'm trying to create dialogue, to spark social change."

KEY TERMS

cultural norms

facilitation

group development

leadership

nonverbal communication

DISCUSSION QUESTIONS

1. How would you describe this group's development? Did they go through recognizable phases? If so, which ones? How do you know?

2. What kinds of cultural norms do you see in this group that are different from a youth group you might see in the U.S.? Give examples. How do these norms influence the process and outcome of the group?

3. What do you think of la lucha, which Jose describes at the end of the case? Why is this value important to Jose? How does this value in social change guide some of the activities this group participated in?

4. What kind of facilitation techniques does Jose use to guide this group? Which, if any, of these techniques do you think could be useful for a group you are participating in?

PART *Group Climate and Relational Communication*

SEEKING RECOVERY THROUGH ONLINE SOCIAL SUPPORT

Laura D. Russell and Tennley A. Vik

Members of an online support group discuss their struggles with eating disorders and deal with the changing membership of their group.

Stepping off the scale, Kat sighed while standing still, cold, and flustered. She looked up into the bathroom mirror to see the noticeable darkness beneath her eyes. "How do I let this happen?" Kat murmured while gazing at her reflection. Sifting through the clutter throughout her dorm room, Kat slowly made her way to the computer. She sat down and typed in her password to log onto her online support community to see if anyone had replied to her latest post. Indeed, two people had left responses:

> Leslie: what are you worried about hun?
>
> Jess: are you losing weight?

Kat pondered and then typed:

> Kat: I don't know … I'm not trying to lose weight. I just know that I must be losing because of how things are right now. I'm not eating very much, but I'm honestly not hungry. I'm just so out of energy to do anything. I stand up and get fuzzy vision for a bit and I have no idea as to why. It may have something to do with having to go home for winter break.

Kat glanced at the clock—2:30 a.m. She then saw her schoolbooks, untouched since she arrived back at the dorm for the evening. "Oh no," she thought, "a final exam tomorrow that I haven't even begun to study for . . . I can't even think now. How come I do this to myself?"

*****

Like many college students, Kat struggles with body weight and eating issues. Since an early age, Kat has dealt with anorexia, which continues to present challenges in her daily life. After finding a small online group of others who share similar experiences, Kat frequently turns to her online journal to express and make sense of her personal dilemmas with others. In turn, Kat comments in others' journals, particularly those of members who regularly follow her own postings. This journaling activity takes place through an online social support community, *In Change*, designed for individuals seeking support for recovery.

Like many social support websites, *In Change* has a number of features for members to explore. In particular, the online discussions take place in two specific domains: community forums and individual members' journals. The community forums involve all users posting responses to general questions and concerns about eating disorders and recovery. The members' journal discussions, however, tend to include conversations that circulate among smaller groups of users over time. Typically, more personal information is disclosed in journals; therefore, these discussions tend to attract the journaler's online friends who follow and comment back-and-forth with the journaler over time. While Kat occasionally participates in the community forum, she most often relies on the small group support received through her interactive journal.

*****

While driving home to spend her winter break away from school, Kat dreaded seeing her family and hearing their constant questioning. As she pulled into the driveway, Kat sat in her car taking in the quiet moment before going inside. "I don't have the energy for this," she thought to herself as she slowly stepped out to gather her bags. "Mom's gonna take one look at me and just assume I'm sick again. Family—they just don't understand."

Greeting her at the front door, Kat's mother asked, "How was the drive, sweetie?"

Dropping her bags on the sofa, Kat replied, "The drive was okay. You know, the usual rush hour stuff."

"How were your exams?"

"Oh, fine."

"Fine?"

"Yeah, fine," Kat said as she walked over to the fridge and reached for a bottle of water.

"I just remember that your midterms didn't go so well. I mean, your grades. You think you were able to bring those up?"

"I hope so, but I won't know for sure until we get our grade reports."

"How about some food? There's some leftover casserole in the fridge that I can heat up for you."

"I'm not really hungry, just thirsty," Kat replied while sipping from the water bottle in her hand.

"You look tired. Why don't you try eating something? What can I get for you? We have some yogurt. I know you like yogurt. And I just bought some fresh grapes yesterday."

"Mom, I'm fine. I'm just not hungry right now."

"I'm worried about you, dear. You're pale. Have you been losing weight?"

Kat paused while looking at the floor, feeling tension and frustration inside. This conversation was like déjà vu—the same thing every time she went home. In all of her past efforts to explain her struggles, Kat knew her family would never understand her anxiety and fear around food. Even when Kat was improving, her small efforts were not always visibly present to others. Therefore, her family tended to draw attention to indicators of her being "sick" and was often blinded to seeing the gradual ways in which she had been improving her life. It was this ongoing tension that Kat experienced in family misunderstandings that initially led her to seek online support. Upon finding a group of others who also lived with eating disorders, Kat discovered comfort in talking about her problems with people who understood her with little need for explanation. Her worries, fears, and concerns—which seemed foreign to her family members—were validated, affirmed, and openly discussed with her online friends who frequently commented in her journal. This online space was like an escape to a world where Kat could feel normal again.

Catching herself in the gaze of her mother, Kat fought to temper the anger she felt inside.

"Mom, why is this the first conversation we have every time I come home? Can't you just be happy to see me?" Kat questioned as she grabbed her bags and began heading upstairs.

"I'm just worried about you being away from home and sick. I want to help you, Kat. Just let me help you."

*****

Kat walked into her room, tossed her bags into the corner, and sat down at the computer. After logging online, she visited her journal and added:

> Kat: I don't know why but my home is possibly the biggest trigger in the world for me. You wouldn't think so, since the bad things that happened in it are years in the past. But somehow I find that my struggles come flooding back when I visit my parents. I don't feel like I can eat here. I try, but it just feels so wrong inside.

After typing, Kat sighed in the relief of releasing her tensions through journaling. She then read others' journal entries for the day and paused when coming across a post made by her friend, Sarah:

> Sarah: Sometimes I feel like such a hypocrite. I try to help people on here and write encouraging things. But then when it comes to my own life I really have a hard time. Like, I go throughout the day and think that people are counting on me—how come that doesn't always seem to be enough? I love you all, but recovery is just becoming so hard. Do any of you feel this way?

"Wow," Kat thought. "That's exactly how I feel." In response, Kat replied to Sarah:

> Kat: I feel that way a lot. Today I was trying to eat dinner with my family and just looking at my plate made me nervous. I so badly just want to give up and not feel like I always have to fight. But I do think about what I write on here and I want to be able to do the same things that I encourage others to do. It's just not that easy. Family has a way of turning everything upside down.

After posting her response, Kat sat feeling the rush of the day quickly catching up with her. With her heavy eyes, even the computer screen appeared blurry. "What a day," she murmured after logging off the computer and making her way to bed. "Sometimes I just wish I had them here with me to talk . . . it would be so different," Kat thought to herself, longing to meet the people with whom she shared the feelings that she kept secret from everyone else in her life.

While Kat's friends were like family, it was often difficult to only have contact with this group online. In particular, waiting for responses from others took time; whereas some friends would reply within hours, others would take days to respond. Therefore, at times when Kat needed immediate support, she could not depend on her online friends to be present. Hence, while online journaling provided a convenient way to stay in touch, its asynchronous structure limited members' abilities to get prompt feedback from others. It was also hard to ask questions that might more readily emerge and be responded to in an everyday conversation. For instance, when Kat received numerous responses to her journal entries, it took considerable time for her to reply to everyone's individual comments. There were times when she simply could not respond to everyone. In such cases, Kat worried that others might think she was either ignoring or being inconsiderate of their offered support. These dilemmas aside, Kat was grateful to at least have this online group to which she felt she belonged. "Guess I should at least be happy I found them online—can't imagine how I'd go through this without them," she thought as she slowly closed her eyes and fell asleep.

******

Kat and her friends often exchanged stories when writing back and forth. It was their way of voicing their struggles while simultaneously creating a sense of hope for each other. Through narrating their experiences together, this journaling group worked through personal problems and affirmed one another's difficult confessions.

The discussion thread for Sarah's journal continued as Leslie joined in with a reply:

> Leslie: Kat, I know you've been going through a difficult time with your family right now. I understand your struggles too, Sarah. My situation is a little different, I guess, since I'm a mom. I feel like a hypocrite every day with my kids. I'm telling them to do healthy things all the while having trouble being healthy myself. But like you, it's not about what I look like but about how difficult the pain is on the inside that I'm fighting.

Leslie, who had been in recovery longer than other members of the group, was often respected as a leader. She had experienced a number of situations that other members were encountering for the first time. As such, Leslie always had advice and personal insight to offer when encouraging others.

*****

When Kat awoke the next day she read Leslie's comment and began thinking about how families complicate things. She wrote:

> Kat: I can't imagine what it must be like to be a mom in your position. Family seems to add a whole other layer to my problems. I want them to think that I'm healthy. Like my mom, she worries all the time and that just makes me feel worse.

Within nearly ten minutes, Leslie had replied:

> Leslie: I know what you mean Kat. Family is something we all struggle with. But I try to think about my getting better not so much as something to please other people. I want to be happy with myself. You deserve to be better for you.

While reading the reply, Kat felt her stomach gnawing with hunger. The feeling of emptiness was both familiar and strange. Yet Leslie's words appearing on the screen lingered in Kat's mind—*you deserve to be better for you.* "She's right," Kat thought. "I've got to do this for myself." Kat recalled the posted comments she received from her friends online. "I can't let them down," Kat asserted. "We're fighting this together. I have to keep fighting."

*****

Scrolling to other parts of the website, Kat clicked on her personal journal and found a reply from one of her friends. Commenting on Kat's expressed struggles with her family, Marybeth responded:

> Marybeth: It makes sense for your house to be a trigger for you. If that is the place where your eating disorder manifested and if that is where your behaviors frequently took place, you're going to remember that.
>
> I too have a hard time at home. My parents got divorced when I was in high school and at that point in my life things seemed crazy. There has been tension in the house since then and so I find comfort in creating stability by controlling my eating patterns. As bad as they might be, they feel right and help me feel more able to take on the day. I feel strong in my recovery now, but going home is still a persisting challenge. I totally understand how you feel.

As this online group continued to share stories with one another, they created meaningful understandings of recovery and the struggles it entails. Kat identified with Marybeth's reply. "She always seems to understand," Kat thought as she began to write back:

> Kat: Thanks Marybeth. I'm so glad you understand me. It seems like lately no one understands what it's like to recover when the world can be so demanding. I wish I knew how

to help people get a sense of how I feel, but they just don't get it. My mom still sees me as sick, and my dad thinks I'm a failure. I'm getting better, but to everyone else that means miraculous weight gain. There's so much more to recovery that people can't see. I even think people on the rest of this site are becoming a little shallow. I've just been staying with the journals lately because that's where most of my friends are. I care less about the forum.

Kat shared much more of her personal self with the friends she developed through her interactive journal than with members participating in online forums. Those who followed Kat's journal entries had developed an ongoing relationship with her that provided the opportunity for them to discuss their more deeply rooted issues and feelings. Lacking this personal depth, the community forum left Kat feeling less satisfied when compared to the discussions she experienced through journaling with her small group of friends. She trusted her journaling partners in a way that allowed her to feel safe sharing herself openly and honestly. Even in times when she experienced relapse, this group of friends always seemed to understand and provided encouraging words.

*****

Weeks passed throughout Kat's winter break. Between family travel and holiday gatherings, Kat was away from the computer. She missed her online friends and looked forward to having a chance to catch up with them. It was the day after Christmas when Kat finally had a moment to log onto *In Change*. Reading through everyone's replies and stories, Kat clicked on Leslie's journal to find a discussion for which she had not prepared herself:

> Sarah: Hi Leslie. I haven't heard from you in a while and just wondered how things were going. I hope you had a good Christmas. Let us know what's up!

> Marybeth: Leslie, where are you girl? How are the kids? We're all thinking about you. Write when you have a chance.

> Sarah: Alright, it's now been a week and you haven't let me know about things. I hope that you're doing okay. We need to catch up girl!

Kat continued to scroll down through several replies to find a shocking post by Leslie:

> Leslie: Thanks for all of your concerns. I'm going through a difficult time right now and have been doing terrible with my eating. Recovery had been going well for so long that I didn't realize my old habits creeping up on me. I can't be here anymore with you, it wouldn't be right. I'm not strong enough. Recovery is just not for me now.

Kat froze, reading the post over and over again. *Leslie's not strong enough? Leaving?* The words flooded her mind as she wrestled to understand how this could be happening. Leslie, the one who always had the right things to say, the one who always found strength in the most difficult times—leaving. "What am I going to do without her . . . what are *we* going to do without her?" Kat questioned, staring blankly at the screen.

KEY TERMS

building relationships   group identity

computer-mediated communication   roles

group boundaries   social support

DISCUSSION QUESTIONS

1. Thinking about Kat's experience, how could the bona fide group perspective help us make sense of the different groups she is part of? Where do you see shifting boundaries in group membership?

2. Based on your experiences, how does group climate affect communication online? What kind of climate do you think this group has? What communication contributes to this climate?

3. How do group or individual roles influence communication climate? In this specific case, how might the group roles and climate influence members' goals to seek support and recovery?

4. How does the use of technology enable and constrain this group's ability to meet its goals?

5. Do you think having a support group online would initiate different expectations for group roles/group climate than would be expected in face-to-face settings? How?

6. What happens in groups when a leader or other powerful group member leaves the group? What suggestions would you have for Kat and the other members of this support group after Leslie's departure?

case 10

GETTING A "W"[1]

Paul Kang and David R. Seibold

A successful varsity basketball team develops a competitive climate and manages conflict between players as they prepare for an important game.

"You guys need to have more ownership of your team. We're going to let you come up with three things that you still need to work on in order to finish the season on a strong note," Head Coach Baker declared. With that the coaching staff left the team room.

When the coaches returned, players had written four items on the board: "rebound," "play consistently for forty minutes," "continue to stay humble and hungry," and "TEAM." Each point had been emphasized by the coaching staff throughout the season. Three of the veterans, Richard, William, and Patrick, explained the importance of the first three items. Jeff, a newer team member (sophomore) but one of the leading scorers of the team and that week's conference player of the week, rose to explain the last item. He paused briefly.

Then he began drawing two hands on the board—one open hand and the second a fist. Some of the players smiled knowingly.

"Now . . ." Jeff started, mimicking the head coach, "We can either be five individuals or one fist."

The team erupted in laughter and the head coach snickered. The meeting ended and players and coaches left laughing. As the room cleared, one of the staffers erased the board.

When practice ended, the players and coaches huddled in the middle of the court, as they always did. Coach Baker paced inside the huddle and stared at the different players.

---

[1]The following case study contains explicit language. Although this may be offensive and uncomfortable for some readers, the authors decided to include the abrasive language to portray accurately the communication occurring in this sport team. Readers also may wish to reflect on its functions, especially the way it influences how members work together.

"Good practice, guys. Remember now, we need to take care of this game on the road. This is a good challenge for us. If we're going to be the team that gets to the end, we need to continue to take care of business. That's the only way we'll finish the season on top and get a high seed in the tournament," he said sternly.

No one else spoke.

"Bring it in, now!"

Players brought their hands together.

"Cardinals on three. One, two, three," the head coach barked.

"Cardinals!" everyone yelled.

Most of the players started toward the locker room in good spirits. Three players, Parker, William, and Patrick, remained on the court to work on their shooting. The coaching staff chatted as they walked off the court.

"By the way, anyone know when it's supposed to rain?" Head Coach Baker asked.

"I believe the drive up will be okay. But it may come down on game day," Assistant Coach Bronston replied.

"Okay. So we'll leave at 12:30, have sandwiches on the bus, and get there around 5."

"Don't forget to order my usual—the Heart Attack. Hey, Maurer, what time do we have the gym tomorrow night?" Head Coach Baker asked.

"From seven to nine," Assistant Coach Maurer replied.

"All right, see you guys tomorrow."

BACKGROUND

The Ocean Conference is in NCAA Division 1, but it is not a power conference in varsity basketball. Therefore, unlike other conferences (such as Big East or Big 10), only the conference tournament champion is granted an invitation to the NCAA tournament each March. Last season, the Western Coast College Cardinals men's basketball team began the season with a losing record (2–7), but finished strong to close 8–8 in conference play. Their season ended when they lost in the semifinal game of the Ocean Conference tournament.

This year, analysts had the Cardinals finishing second in the conference. Many experts thought the Cardinals' young, talented, and returning players would provide depth and scoring. The team seemed to live up to predictions, winning the first four preconference games. Two of these wins were against teams from bigger conferences. Things went downhill when the team lost its next four games and ended the preseason with a record of 5–5. To make matters worse, the team split its first two regular season games. These ups and downs made players and coaches feel trepidation about which team would show up for the next game. The team then went on a 3–0 run of victories, yet suffered a humiliating loss against a struggling team. The loss was followed by another 3–0 run, then another definitive defeat against another struggling team. Since then, the team seemed to have regained its winning form. They entered the final leg of the season with yet another 4–0 winning streak.

The Cardinals were now scheduled to play a nonconference game against the Central Valley Terriers—part of a sports television network promotion called "Bracket Busters." With the last string of wins, the Cardinals had moved to the top spot in the Ocean Conference and secured a 1- or 2-seed for the conference tournament. They had just won a tough away game and faced three remaining conference games (two home and one away). This game would be against a team from a more powerful conference. Despite their winning record, they were predicted to lose the game by 7.5 points. The coaches also wondered which team would come to play.

THE DAY BEFORE THE GAME

Sandwiches, chips, and bottles of water waited on the bus. With headphones on, players grabbed their rations, sat toward the rear, and began devouring their food right away. Coaches and staff members then entered, grabbed their food, and settled in seats in the front of the bus. Everyone sat alone, but near teammates with whom they felt closest. The African American players, Jeff, Nathan, Patrick, Bill, and Beck, sat in one area. Another group, composed of Philip, William, Parker, Richard, and Jason, were in the last seats. The other three players were dispersed. The players spent much of the five-hour ride listening to music, sleeping, and watching the onboard movie.

During the trip, Assistant Coach Maurer came to a few of the starting players with his laptop. He showed Jeff, Nathan, and Beck additional game footage and discussed strategy with them. Other players were not included in these mini-sessions. With those exceptions, there was little contact between the coaches and the players during the ride. Coaches made occasional small talk with players when needing to stretch or go to the restroom, which was located at the back of the bus.

When the team arrived at the hotel, players were randomly paired up and assigned to rooms.They were then given two hours of free time before practice. Coaches and staff members also shared rooms, with the exception of Coach Baker, who stayed in a room by himself.

Evening Practice

Players and coaches were awed at the enormity of the Terriers' Event Center. But when practice began, it was back to a familiar routine—players started out stretching and then took warm-up shots while quietly joking around. The coaches discussed practice plans and shouted occasional remarks about players needing to be more focused on their tasks. Since the Terriers were considered the more "athletic" team, the head coach wanted to emphasize minimizing turnovers (their last loss came with twenty turnovers) and playing good defense. During several drills Coach Baker stopped the exercise and singled out particular players. He yelled about their lack of intensity during practice as well as the mental mistakes they had made. Other players and the assistant coaches quietly stood in their spots until the rant ended, and then they continued the drill. Today, a senior shooting guard, Patrick, was at the receiving end of a verbal trashing for settling for a three-pointer. Another player was substituted for him, and he stood on the sidelines.

During most drills, players rarely talked to one another. When they did, it was quick and barely audible. The comments often asked for clarification about their role in a particular drill or were made to motivate one another. Assistant coaches stood by some players and offered advice, but these conversations also were quick and hushed—just the way players and coaches had communicated during practices all season.

Also typical of practices throughout the season, players competed against one other. The starting lineup was pitted against the second-string squad during intrasquad drills. Players competed to get "in" on the scrimmages and the drills by demonstrating extra effort or by executing the head coach's orders. Some players would get angry at their teammates. Today it was Patrick, who became upset with Jeff for not correctly executing a play and complained loudly enough for Jeff to hear, but not the coaches. Jeff simply scowled. They continued to jaw at each other throughout the drills.

At the end of practice, Coach Baker had the players sit in the front row of the arena. The assistants sat at the edge or stood to the side. Players quietly watched him as he paced side-to-side while talking.

"Don't take tomorrow's game lightly just because it's a nonconference game. This is an opportunity for you guys to test yourselves against a bigger conference team. While it may not matter to our conference race, winning could be the difference between a 13- and a 14-seed in the NCAA tournament in March. They may have NBA-level talent, but we've got depth and speed and we'll out-hustle them. They only play seven guys. Our guards will pressure their guards. We'll make their post players run. And we'll rotate players faster. We'll be fresh and put constant pressure on them. That's how we'll win! Bring it in."

Players left their seats and huddled.

"Cardinals!"

Dinner

As usual, the coaches did not eat with the players. Bronston, the operations director, took the players to a local restaurant and gave them food allowances. As other patrons gawked, team members settled into their seats, sitting next to their buddies. During dinner, the players talked freely without the fear of repercussions from the coaching staff. Topics included school, video games, parties, movies, but mostly girls. There was little discussion about the upcoming game.

When girls were not the topic, players played practical jokes on one another. Jason threw pieces of balled-up paper at Parker, who was not watching.

"Hey, whoever's doing that s***, you need to quit it. Is it you, Jason?"

Jason looked surprised. Several teammates snickered and also took shots at him.

"Parker's getting mad again."

"It's the Parker show!"

On the other side of the table, Nathan ate all his appetizers without sharing. Jeff reacted.

"What the . . . ?"

"Didn't know you didn't get any." Nathan laughed while chewing the last fried calamari.

"Okay, I see how it is . . ."

Jeff glared at Nathan, who ignored him.

GAME DAY

Coach Baker sat quietly and stared at his Starbucks latte. He was concerned. He knew the players were not as focused on this game as he would like. The recent victories seemed to make them complacent again. He needed to ensure they were still focused and driven to win. He also noticed the two steadily solidifying cliques within his team and considered whether it would cause severe rifts. He reflected on his star players, Jeff and Nathan. Both were extremely talented players, yet Jeff had proven to be much the more coachable. Nathan was too temperamental and selfish. Although Nathan had more natural talent, Jeff had become the team's "go to" player. He wondered if Nathan's antics would become detrimental to the team should Jeff continue to become the team's star player. He sighed as the untouched latte continued to lose heat.

Pregame Meal

Coaches joined the players for the pregame meal, but sat at another table entertaining several program boosters. Unlike other meals, the players did not have a choice of food—everyone had spaghetti with chicken. Players still joked around, but they were a lot more careful not to draw the coaches' attention. Jeff and Nathan went at each other again. This time, Nathan aggravated Jeff by making fun of his appearance. When Jeff dismissed the poorly executed joke, Nathan fired back.

"You know you ain't s***. All you got to do is get me the ball and shut the f*** up."

Jeff gritted his teeth and murmured, "S*** . . . you think you can talk to me like that. We'll see, mother****."

Beck tapped Jeff and whispered, "He's just talkin . . . it ain't s***."

Jeff nodded but did not respond. The table became silent—no one spoke for some time. Assistant Coach Jacobs looked over to see if everything was all right, but didn't catch the low-volume, high-intensity exchange.

The Game

Players quietly prepared for the game while the coaching staff paced around the locker room whispering game strategy among themselves. Jeff and Nathan sat as far away from each other as possible. When it was nearly time to take the floor, Coach Baker got everyone's attention.

"All right. We went over everything and know what you need to do to be successful tonight. You need to go into this game the same as every other game—same preparation, same focus, same hunger . . ."

Players listened intently.

"You know what they like to do. So it's on you to step up and get the job done. You can't get rattled, and you especially can't get punked! You need to play with focus and confidence! Now let's go out there and take care of business!"

Players got up to huddle.

"Cardinals on three. One, two, three . . ."

"Cardinals!"

Players raced out. Coaches followed.

First Half

Jeff and Nathan began poorly. They missed open shots, turned the ball over, and made critical errors on the defensive end. As a result, both players were taken out after just five minutes of play. However, the Cardinals were enjoying an early double-digit lead thanks to some brilliant play by others. The backup center, Stewart, had three blocks, two rebounds, and two dunks in just five minutes, which surpassed his per-game average. The guards also contributed, hitting three-point buckets. What's more, two of the Terriers' top scorers got into early foul trouble and had to sit out most of the first half.

But Coach Baker knew he needed his star players to step up if they were going to get the "W." He kneeled in front of Jeff, who had his head covered with a towel.

"What's going on?"

Jeff did not respond.

"You're not playing like yourself. You're just going through the motions."

Still no response.

"Now listen. If you want this 'W,' you need to snap out of it and play like you're capable of playing. You got it?"

Jeff nodded.

"Get in there for William."

Jeff returned to the game and hit his next two shots—a three-pointer and a layup. Nathan watched from the bench.

Nathan continued to struggle on both ends when he returned, forcing shots in an attempt to match Jeff's performance and losing rebound battles. When the half-time buzzer sounded, the Cardinals' early fifteen-point lead had shrunk to four points.

Second Half

The Cardinals did not score a field goal for the first five minutes of the second half. Luckily, the Terriers also struggled as three starters were in foul trouble. Then Jeff came to life. In one out-of-bounds play, Beck saw him cutting down the lane and threw a high lob-pass. Jeff came down with a thundering dunk that silenced the crowd. The Cardinals' bench erupted in a roaring cheer. The Terriers called a time-out, and the Cardinals ran out to chest-bump Jeff.

Stewart also continued to play well, especially on the defensive end. He rejected eight shots (personal best and new school record) and hindered the opponents with his 7' 9" wingspan. The guards also contributed—hitting timely three-pointers to secure the slim lead.

With three minutes remaining, the Cardinals had a five-point lead. Then Nathan made back-to-back errors. He did not box-out properly, and his opponent tipped in a basket. On the following play, he miscommunicated with Beck and turned over the ball. One of the opposing players hit a short jumper to cut the lead to one point. The home crowd roared, the band blared, and the cheerleaders were jumping up and down. Coach Baker called a time-out with just over two minutes left.

"Nate, you need to cut to the middle of the key on that play and give a passing lane," William yelled at him while the coaching staff stood off to the side conferring about what to do next.

"Shut the f*** up!" Nate yelled.

"Don't tell me to shut the f*** up, you're gonna f****** cost us the game!"

Nate stood up from his chair, glaring at William, and other players grabbed him.

"Let go! And no one f****** talk to me!"

By the time Coach Baker entered the huddle, all the players were silent.

"What the f*** is going on? Is someone going to tell me what's going on!?"

"Nothing, coach . . . just arguing about the play before," Jason offered.

"Well, cut that s*** out. Now, here's what we're going to do . . ."

The game continued to go back and forth, with the Cardinals maintaining a two-point lead. With seven seconds left, William, who had just gotten into it with Nathan, made a critical turnover while trying to inbound the ball. The Terriers called a time out, the crowd went wild, and the public address system blared the song "The Final Countdown." The Cardinals bench was quiet. William got occasional taps on his shoulder, but no one spoke to him.

"Everyone get into the grill of your man. And don't give anyone an open look."

With the crowd standing, the Terriers inbounded the ball to Brian, their top player. He cut across the top of the key and released the ball from behind the three-point line. The shot floated across the noise-filled air and hit the back of the iron. Jeff grabbed the rebound. He was fouled immediately and, with one second left on the clock, sank both free throws. The Cardinals walked off the floor with a four-point "W."

Postgame

"This was a great win for us, and another lesson for us. Jeff did not start well, but picked it up and finished a great game. Stewart, Patrick, and Beck really came through for us today, especially when our usual options did not work. . . . And lastly, William."

Coach Baker paused. "If we had lost the game, you would have never made it as a lawyer. . . . In fact, you would have needed a lawyer."

Coaches and players laughed, William did not.

"Okay, so get changed and then go get some food. Those of you who are eating with your families, let Bronston know before you leave with them."

It was past 10 p.m. and starting to rain as the bus left the Event Center. None of the coaches were aboard—they were celebrating with program boosters. Jeff and a few other players opted to eat with their families. The only players on the bus were those without other options—Stewart, William, Nathan, and several others. They sat by themselves and listened to music. No one talked. The bus stopped at a fast-food restaurant.

"Guys, we don't have a lot of time, so get your food to go. You'll have to eat in your hotel rooms," Bronston ordered.

Players received their $10 food allowances. As they lined up at the counter, some discussed whether they could manage to get a dessert. Nathan and William ordered meals, but did not speak otherwise. When everyone had his food, they trudged onto the bus and returned to the hotel. It continued to rain.

competition

conflict

diversity

task and relational communication

teamwork

roles

patterns of language

DISCUSSION QUESTIONS

1. Although the Cardinals are a group of collegiate varsity basketball players that everyone refers to as a team, do you believe they act and interact as a "team"? Discuss your answer in terms of what you believe a "team' is.

2. What do you think are the most critical issues this team needs to address? How would you go about addressing and resolving these issues? (HINT: Also consider the events that did not occur in this case study that you think ought to happen on a sports team. Notice that some coaches and players were seldom mentioned and did not seem as critical . . .)

3. Discuss the relevance of the head coach and assistant coaches to the team. Should they be considered part of the team? Why or why not?

4. The notion of competition is firmly entrenched in the minds of the players. How is this beneficial *and* detrimental to the team?

5. What do you notice about the team when they are "on" and "off" the court? How does one affect the other (and vice versa)?

6. Discuss the relevance of relationships (or lack thereof) on this team. Discuss the implications.

7. If you were being recruited to play for the Cardinals, and given what you know now, would you want to be a part of the team? Why or why not?

"I CAN HAS COMMUNITY?"

Norms and Social Support in a lolcat Fan Group

Michelle Calka

Members of an online group celebrate their birthdays, support one another, and discuss how to respond to "trolls" in their community.

Mary[1] sat down at the small kitchen table in her Winnebago motor home and opened her laptop. Since her retirement two years ago, Mary and her husband had decided that it was time to see more of the country, so they packed up their belongings, sold their home, and took off in their Winnie. They had been on the road since then, and while Mary loved the bonding time with her husband and the travel, she often missed her family and friends back home. It was a relief that she had found the lolcat online community of icanhascheezburger.com[2] several years ago, or she might have been driven insane by her husband.

Mary knew that many people might find her online hobby strange, and maybe even call her a crazy cat lady. Lolcats are user-submitted pictures of cats with funny captions attached to them, usually with poor grammar and spelling.[3] The caption is often from the perspective of the cat; it is assumed that if cats could speak and write, they would certainly reject the constraints of good grammar. While Mary enjoyed looking at the lolcats, this was not her primary purpose for being here. For some people, lolcats might have seemed childish, silly, or a waste of time, but Mary found much more within this website. Underneath each picture was a message board for users to leave comments about the picture or anything else on their mind. In the two years since the site had opened, hundreds of individuals had registered on

---

[1]Online user names have been changed.

[2]Often abbreviated "ICHC." The first lolcat was a picture of a large grey cat gazing with a comically hungry expression at what one assumes is a cheeseburger off-camera, with the caption "I can has cheezburger?"

[3]See Figure 1 for an example.

FIGURE 1—*Example of lolcat*

the boards. While the asynchronous[4] discussions sometimes talked about cats or the pictures, the hundreds of comments under each picture often turned very personal. Mary had gotten to know a core group of about a dozen users quite well, and she considered them her friends. Over the years, she had even met several of them offline.

In order to better accommodate this smaller community of "cheezfriends," Mary had created a blog for personal updates and events in "cheezland," the virtual space of the icanhascheezburger message boards. Part of her job was to read the message boards to find these updates and then copy them to the blog, so the group could find the information quickly and easily. She also received regular e-mail contact from some of the members, which she shared on the blog. The group found this to be a much more organized way to set up online birthday parties and other fun events like virtual snowball fights (which required a good bit of imagination), as well as sharing more personal health and family updates. While the events happened on the main icanhascheezburger message board, it was useful to have a smaller, quieter place to read the community's news.

As she logged onto the website, Mary was a bit concerned for her friends; several members of the group were ill or going through major life changes, and she was eager for updates on them. She was pleased with the positive climate the group had created;

---

[4]Asynchronous online communication is not immediate; there is a time lapse between messages, unlike online chat. Message replies are threaded to clarify who is responding to which posted message.

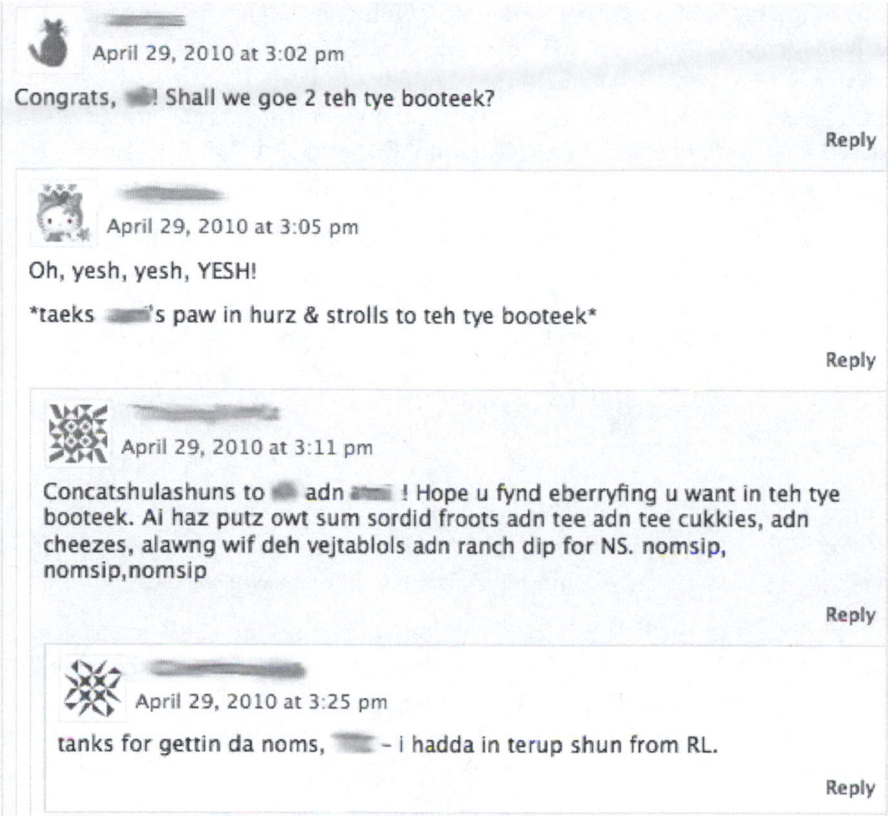

April 29, 2010 at 3:02 pm

Congrats, ▬! Shall we goe 2 teh tye booteek?

Reply

April 29, 2010 at 3:05 pm

Oh, yesh, yesh, YESH!

taeks ▬'s paw in hurz & strolls to teh tye booteek

Reply

April 29, 2010 at 3:11 pm

Concatshulashuns to ▬ adn ▬! Hope u fynd eberryfing u want in teh tye booteek. Ai haz putz owt sum sordid froots adn tee adn tee cukkies, adn cheezes, alawng wif deh vejtablols adn ranch dip for NS. nomsip, nomsip,nomsip

Reply

April 29, 2010 at 3:25 pm

tanks for gettin da noms, ▬ - i hadda in terup shun from RL.

Reply

FIGURE 2—*Screenshot of threaded discussion and lolspeak*

members felt comfortable talking about these issues and receiving virtual "head scritches," paw squeezes, and "beams," or good thoughts from others. There was an interesting metaphoric crossover of people as cats and cats as people, but these imaginative aspects were fun and brought them together over a common interest in cats.

Mary smiled at the new lolcat pictures, but she was more interested in the threaded comments below. She scanned the postings for updates on her friends, and then copied them over to the blog.

"Janet b due tu hab SirJury on her borkt finner. Meg (hopefully) had SirJury on her-borkt anklol last nite. KCT is rekuvvering frum knee replaismint SirJury. Catz'z pop-in-law may b removinged frum life support. Emily wuz habbing wut may haz ben a gall bladder attakk last nite."

Janet is due to have surgery on her borked (broken) finger. Meg (hopefully) had surgery on her borked ankle last night. KCT is recovering from knee replacement surgery. Catz's father-in-law may be removed from life support. Emily was having what may have been a gall bladder attack last night.

Some of the comments were written in lolspeak,[5] while some were written in standard English. Mary usually just copied the text of whatever was in the post, or summarized it in lolspeak if it was a particularly long post. Sometimes members would e-mail Mary updates to post to the blog, which made her life easier. Mary had become quite adept at translating text to lolspeak; she considered it a fun hobby and a type of communication skill. While lolspeak was not a requirement for posting, Mary thought that it did help to create a sense of community.

Mary noticed that there were also some new developments on the boards to share with others:

> "Bluesfanz mahm fawl down go boom … It tuked fereber butt tehy gived hur a CT skan, teh noggin iz otay, sum stiches, hur pour eye iz awl brewsed an swelled shut an tehy gived hur a chest xrai an nuffing iz borked, thanx CC. Cud haz bean mush mush wurse."

Bluesfan's mom fell down. It took forever but they gave her a CT scan, the noggin is okay, some stitches, her poor eye is all bruised and swelled shut and they gave her a chest X-ray and nothing is borked, thank Ceiling Cat. Could have been much much worse.

As updates were posted to the blog, other members responded with messages of support and sympathy. There was happy news to post, too: One member was "adopted" by a stray dog, another was planning a "happy divorce" party, and a "cheezmeet" was in the works, where several of the members would get together in person. Mary was excited about catching up with her friends online and having the opportunity to meet some new members in person. It was strange, Mary thought, to feel so close to people without really knowing what their lives are like.

Mary scrolled to the next lolcat image. "Hmm, there seem to be a lot more comments than usual on this one," she thought to herself. She had only been away from the boards for a day while they traveled; had she really missed that much? As she scrolled through the thread, she swore silently to Basement Cat.[6] A troll[7] had incited a flame war[8] on the message boards. Mary never understood why trolls seemed to get so much satisfaction out of posting malicious comments and calling others names. Icanhascheezburger had a good little community going, Mary thought, and they did not need this kind of trouble. Many of the nasty postings and responses had already been removed by the time Mary opened the

---

[5]Lolspeak is the preferred language of icanhascheezburger for both captions and message postings. It is similar to regular English, but with alternate verb conjugations and spellings. Over time, many of these grammatical forms have become standardized within the community.

[6]Basement Cat is the lolcat equivalent of the devil and the nemesis of Ceiling Cat, or the lolcat equivalent of a watchful and benevolent God.

[7]Trolls are individuals who make inflammatory or derogatory comments toward others in order to disrupt the conversation or provoke others into responding. However, posters are sometimes called trolls if they unintentionally violate the norms of the community or express dissenting opinions.

[8]A flame war is a kind of online argument in which users and a troll engage in an extended exchange of negative messages.

thread; the moderators[9] at icanhascheezburger were fairly quick about responding to complaints and banning the user names of those who harassed others. However, there was little to stop the trolls from creating another user name and doing the same thing again, and the urge to respond to them seemed irresistible to the group. Mary knew that something had to be done, but first she had to find out what had happened. She dashed an e-mail off to members Lisa, Pat, and Fadeleaf (three members who did not seem to be dealing with crises in their personal lives) to get their take on the situation and then went to help make dinner.

About an hour later, Mary heard a familiar "ding!" from her laptop. She received responses from Lisa and Pat. Both had similar reactions—she knew it was bad if they were not using lolspeak. Lisa wrote, "Oh, he was the worst I ever saw! Hands down. Just awful. Ugly attitude, mean and nasty, foul language, and he wouldn't go away!" Pat reported, "The troll on Saturday was abusive and as much as said he was there only to antagonize and that any response we gave was getting him off. Which really reflects poorly on this so-called person, but sadly that seems to be the mentality."

Both Lisa and Pat went on to explain what had happened; the troll had called a group member a "retard," and the community jumped to the person's defense, but the troll's comments kept getting more and more offensive. In short, the group was "feeding the trolls." Mary responded back to all three members, expressing her frustration at the situation and the group's response to it.

> "I haz tu agree dat jumping on deh trollz kin sumtimez b berry hard tu resist. But I also noez dat sum uv dem just say thingz tu see wut kind uv reakshun dey will git frum us. And if dey b wanting attenshun, ignoring dem b deh best way tu irritating dem. :evil: So, frum now on, I will due mai utmost to not feed deh trollz."

I have to agree that jumping on the trolls can sometimes be very hard to resist. But I also know that some of them just say things to see what kind of reaction they will get from us. And if they want attention, ignoring them is the best way to irritate them. (evil grin) So from now on, I will do my utmost to not feed the trolls.

About twenty minutes later, as Mary pondered what to do next, Fadeleaf's response popped up in Mary's inbox.

"The troll thing is kinda tough, I think. The idea of ignoring the trolls is sometimes much more easily thought than done. Sometimes they just BEG for a response. When they start attacking us for doing what we do and being who we are (online persona-wise, anyway), I'm not sure responding is entirely inappropriate. One thing I HAVE noticed lately is that sometimes cheezpeeps are a little too quick to label people 'trolls' without any evidence to back up the claims."

---

[9]Moderators are employees of icanhascheezburger who are responsible for monitoring the message boards for inappropriate content.

Mary realized that the other three were online, and so engaged them in an online chat session. Lisa responded to Mary's e-mail in the chat.

> "I agrees with teh no feeding the trolls … but I do like to poke em with a stik onse in a wile. *ebil smirk*"

I agree with not feeding the trolls . . . but I do like to poke them with a stick once in a while (evil smirk).

Fadeleaf responded, "I think cheezpeeps might need to stop every once in a while & realize that not everyone understands our etiquette—especially people who are extremely new to the site and understandably think the 'comments' section would be a sensible place to insert their comments about the current lol. Unless you're familiar with the people who chat there, there's no reason outsiders (I'm not liking that term, but it's the one that's coming to mind and I'm too lazy to come up with a better term) would realize that it has become more of a chat room and less of a place to simply comment on lols. I don't think those people should be jumped upon and immediately harassed. People who come in and say they don't find a particular lol to be amusing (or that a particular lol is offensive in one manner or another) also shouldn't be jumped upon and harassed, IMO (in my opinion)."

Mary could certainly understand where Fadeleaf was coming from. If she had not been a cheezpeep for so long, she could see how it might be weird to find out that very few people on the comments page were actually talking about the lolcat picture. She had also seen many different types of trolls over the years: those who made mean comments and quickly went away, those who did not find the picture funny or were concerned for the safety of the cat in the picture, those who thought the image was altered, those who made fun of individuals for speaking lolspeak. Mary understood that there were many levels of troll, and perhaps some of these people they were calling trolls were just unfamiliar with how the group operated. Was there a "one size fits all" solution to trolls?

Pat suggested, "How about I make a new logo for the boards—we'll call it 'Nil Per Troll' (NPT) or 'Don't Feed the Trolls.' It can be our code phrase to use whenever a troll appears."

"That's a fantastic idea!" Mary thought to herself. She responded,

> "I'm glad you explained it, kuz I duzn't speek deh latin. I duz noe deh dredded R werd b 'retard,' a term I adn menny uzzerz feel shud neber b sed in polite kumpany. If deh trollz (oar enneewun) uzez deh obseen langwidge, dehy shud b reported tu deh Cheezez hoo b running deh ICHC sew deyre commintz can b removinged frum deh site, if deh Cheezez deem dem tu b offensive. Plz tu remember dat dere b a differnse btween irritating adn offensive adn not b buggin deh Cheezez wifowt gud kauze."

I'm glad you explained it, because I don't speak Latin. I do know the dreaded "R" word is "retard," a term I and many others feel should never be said in polite company. If the trolls (or anyone) use obscene language, they should be reported to the Cheezez (the moderators) who run ICHC so their comments can be removed from the site, if the Cheezez deem them to be too offensive. Please remember that there is a difference between irritating and offensive, so don't bug the Cheezez without good cause.

Mary noticed that Fadeleaf was quiet for a while in the chat session. She knew that Fadeleaf was still feeling skeptical when his next message appeared.

"I don't know, guys. The comments section should be both a fun place for chatting by the cheezpeeps (and whomever else wants to pop in) and a safe spot for non-personal drive-by comments from passers-by. I think people who pop in and start insulting ICHC and/or people using lolspeak do so at their own peril. Sometimes jumping all over them is fun."

It was clear to Mary that Pat, Lisa, and Fadeleaf were all correct, even if they did not exactly agree on the best way to handle the troll situation. Mary also knew that it would be her responsibility to make a post to the blog and explain what had happened and what course of action the group was going to advocate. Since all posts went through her, she had control over what messages were posted. She thanked the other group members for giving their opinions and closed the chat session. Mary got up from the kitchen table and poured herself a cup of tea. While she knew that she could not control how other members of the community responded to trolls, her small group of frequent posters could have a big impact on the climate of the message board. If the group could agree on a preferred method for dealing with the trolls, it might be possible to defend against further attacks. She felt that the group had created very positive relationships, and she hated the thought of outsiders coming in and destroying the good climate they had established. At the same time, Fadeleaf raised a good point; how closed off should the group be? Would ignoring anyone who did not meet their established norms discourage new members?

While she now knew the opinion of three of the members, she was not sure how the rest of the group would feel. She needed to make a decision that was somewhere between soliciting further feedback from members or advocating for a course of action to deal with the trolls. She did not know how long it would be until they hit the boards again. She opened up a new blog post window and began typing.

> "Oh hai, peepz!! I b wanting tu tawking tu u bowt deh owtbrake uv trollz wii haz had in cheezland dis past week. Normally, deh peepz hoo b commintting on ICHC b deh kind and frendly peepz. Wii haz awlwayz had deh trollz, tu, tho. Tehre b mennee kindz uv trollz, az u may noe. Most b relativelee harmless, dey just run threw saying sumfing adn den leeveing. Often tehy just think deh pic not b funny or b kunserned fur deh well-being uv deh kitty (care trollz). Adn dere iz nuffing rong wif peepz expressing dere opinyunz. But menny uv us take exsepshun tu deh trollz hoo b kumming tu ICHC tu belittle oar bully peepz. Dis haz kunserned sevral peepz, maisef inkluded. Wii haz pondered dis subject via deh emayoz."

Oh hi, people. I want to talk to you about the outbreak of trolls we've had in cheezland (the ICHC boards) this past week. Normally, the people who comment on ICHC are kind and friendly people. We have always had the trolls too, though. There are many kinds of trolls, as you may know. Most are relatively harmless, they just run through saying something and then leaving. Often they just think the picture is not funny or are concerned for the well-being of the kitty (care trolls). And there is nothing wrong with people expressing their opinions. But many of us take exception to the trolls who come to ICHC to belittle or bully people. This has concerned several people, myself included. We have pondered this subject via e-mail.

Mary took a deep breath and another sip of tea, still thinking about what she was going to say next.

KEY TERMS

computer-mediated communication	group climate
decision making	group identity
conflict	norms

DISCUSSION QUESTIONS

1. What norms are being enacted or created within this group?

2. This group is struggling with the distinction between new members who are unfamiliar with the norms and trolls with malicious intent. How does this process work with other groups? How can group members acclimate new members in a way that does not disrupt the functioning of the community?

3. How does the unique language of lolspeak create and reinforce group identity? What are some examples of unique words or language in other groups that you know of?

4. What is the potential impact of negative communication on this group's climate? What might happen to the group if they did not address the issue of trolls?

5. How does the asynchronous nature of message board posting and email affect communication in this situation? Is this a positive or a negative effect?

6. If you were in Mary's situation, what would you say to the community?

PART

Conflict in Groups

A Matter of Respect

Mary Meares

A manager tries to decide how to deal with cultural conflict between two members of her work team.

Amy sighed. As the executive director and CEO of a small international nonprofit organization, International Culture Partners (ICP), she usually loved her job. She had joined the organization in its infancy because she cared about the mission—to educate employees of aid agencies, nonprofits, corporations, and governmental organizations about cultural differences and help them to be more effective. The organization had been a great fit with her ideals. She had wanted, and still did want, to make the world a better place, to help professionals to learn about other cultures so that they could better provide services for their clients and customers. While housed in the United States, ICP had always attracted employees of different nationalities and backgrounds. The organization had started with a small but diverse core of young employees who worked together, played together, and felt that they really did make a contribution. It was an exciting place to be and everyone shared a passion for the work.

In fact, Amy still felt that the organization was making a difference; it was just harder and harder to manage the staff. In the early days, they had been more like a family, working together and supporting each other. When had things gotten so out of hand? It was still a small team, only seven year-round employees plus other part-time and temporary workers who came in when things got busy with conferences and workshops. The employees were still idealistic and motivated by the mission. What had changed was the atmosphere in the office and the dissension among the staff, especially between two of her key employees. When Amy looked back, it seemed to her that over the last three years, as ICP had gotten more successful and busy, team morale had disintegrated.

Amy thought back to a conversation she had had that morning with Helga, the staff accountant. Helga was from Germany, but had been living in the United States for twenty years. Helga was one of the original employees, and she and Amy had been friends from the beginning. Her business focus and task orientation had always been a blessing for ICP—she got the work done when it needed to be done and had helped ICP stay afloat in the early days. She worked closely with all of the other members of the group. Unfortunately, Helga was having a problem with another staff member, Mariana, a young Brazilian, who worked as a staff assistant for programming, helping to arrange seminars, workshops, and conferences.

Just this morning, Helga had turned to Amy and said, "I just can't take it anymore—it's a matter of respect. Mariana doesn't respect my time or the expertise I've gained over the last ten years doing this work. I don't care what everyone else is doing as long as they get their work done on time and cooperate; I just want to get my work done. But every time I get immersed in my tasks, she interrupts me! That just doesn't cut it when you're handling money and can't make any mistakes."

Mariana had started as an intern while she was earning her master's degree, but had returned to work as a full-time employee after she graduated the following year. Amy liked to give potential employees a chance to prove themselves by starting out in a less permanent role, and Mariana had been an excellent intern. She was very smart, organized, and responsible. When she came back as an employee, she quickly became part of the team. In the four years she had worked at ICP she had completely reorganized the office. Amy thought she was a wonderful addition to the staff. Mariana could take on coordination of projects, did not need much supervision, and had high standards for excellent work. In fact, some other members of the group would grumble when she criticized them for not maintaining her high level of expectations. She was increasingly given the responsibility for working with executive clients and serving as a team leader, coordinating the work of other members. Amy was concerned to hear that the antagonism between two of her most responsible and productive team members was increasing.

When Amy asked for more specifics about what Mariana did, Helga said, "Well, sometimes she offers to help me, but she doesn't have accounting skills and with money, you have to be very careful. Then other times, she asks me if I need anything . . . really—I just need to be left alone. She's trying to brown-nose with me and wants everyone to like her, but really, I think she wants to take over. I don't trust her at all. She drives me crazy!" Amy began to worry, but her conversation with Helga was interrupted by a phone call from a client.

That afternoon, the ICP staff members had their regularly scheduled staff meeting. Amy was excited to share news of a new international training contract with the staff. When she asked who wanted to be on the project implementation team, Mariana jumped in to volunteer. She added, "Helga would be great, too, but she's so busy with other projects we'll have to survive without her." Amy was surprised; Mariana sounded as if she was sincerely disappointed that they couldn't work together. Amy mentioned that, as the staff accountant, Helga's expertise would definitely be needed. Mariana countered, "We can always consult with her if financial questions come up, but we can muddle through if we need to. We have to be respectful of her time." Helga crossed her arms in front of her chest and said nothing. As soon as the meeting was over, she walked briskly out of the room without saying anything to anyone, went in her office, and closed the door.

Amy asked Mariana to stay after the meeting to touch base on another project, but she really wanted to ask about the staff problem. While initially reluctant to talk about the tensions between her and Helga, Mariana opened up, saying, "I really respect Helga. She's been here a long time and I know you really trust her. But she is so disrespectful towards me! She acts like she doesn't trust me, plus she can be so abrasive! I try to be nice to her, to develop good rapport, but she just snaps at me. I get along with everyone else here, but it seems like Helga is sabotaging me and trying to get everyone else here on her side. Jeff and I hang out together after work and Akiko is very sweet, but I think the others are being poisoned against me. Please, Amy, know that I am trying very hard to get her to like me for the sake of the team, but it seems like a lost cause. I thought it would just be better if she was not part of the team for that reason."

As work was wrapping up in the office for the day, Amy had a chance to talk to three other members of the team about the situation. Akiko, Jack, and Jeff were waiting for a response from a client and were reminiscing about how they had gotten interested in working with ICP. When Amy came by, she asked them what they thought of Helga and Mariana's working relationship and how it affected them as team members.

Akiko was an international graduate student intern at ICP. Her answer was vague: "I love working at ICP. It's a wonderful opportunity for me, but the United States is very different from Japan. Some of the behavior that I see, well, it's not what we would do in Japan. Helga is very kind to me—she helped me to get this internship. And Mariana is very friendly—she always talks to me. I like being part of the team. Sometimes, though, working at this office is very difficult for me."

Jack, a middle-aged American, said, "I just want to focus on my tasks for the team and our mission, but both Helga and Mariana keep pressuring me to take their side. Just yesterday, I was working with Mariana, She said that she 'needed my support,' but really she just wanted me to take her side over Helga's. Later in the afternoon Helga checked in with me to make sure I wasn't turning against her. They act like this is high school when they're both adults. I refuse to take sides, but still get sucked in with it all. It makes it stressful for everyone on the team."

Jeff, an American thirty-something, was much more blunt. "Here's the story. Helga is used to being in charge and being your right hand. She's threatened by Mariana because Mariana works hard and everyone likes her. Helga is afraid Mariana is going to take her place in the hierarchy. It's kind of a joke—there isn't really a hierarchy anyway. We all work as part of the team. I've told Mariana that she should sit down and talk to Helga, but she says that she doesn't feel comfortable confronting her and doesn't want to be disrespectful. I wish Helga could just have some respect for Mariana and the rest of us, too!"

That evening after everyone else had left, Amy sat in her office and tried to figure out what she could do. Helga and Mariana both had too much history and were too good as employees to fire them, but how could they get past the problems? How could the organization teach others about cultural differences when they could not get along themselves? You can't force people to respect each other, can you? What is respect, anyway?

KEY TERMS

conflict style   group climate

culture   leadership

diversity

DISCUSSION QUESTIONS

1. What is respect? What concrete behaviors do you believe are respectful and which are disrespectful?

2. How does a group member's background and experience influence their evaluation of respect and disrespectful behavior?

3. In what ways is Marianna being respectful? In what ways is she being disrespectful?

4. In what ways is Helga being respectful? In what ways is she being disrespectful?

5. How is Marianna and Helga's conflict impacting the rest of the group? What should or can other group members do about this situation?

6. What should a group member who feels disrespected do? Who is responsible for resolving this behavior?

7. How can you minimize the potential for disrespectful behavior in groups?

case 13

CONFLICT ON CORE SOUND

Understanding the Influence of Goal Conflict on Group Decision Making during a Sea Kayaking Expedition

Bruce Martin and Levi Dexel

A kayaking expedition changes course after group members experience difficulty on the water.

As they loaded their kayaks in preparation for their second day of paddling, Patrick, the designated leader of the day, informed the group of the travel goal for the day. "My plan for the day is to cross Core Sound and make up the miles that we lost yesterday!" The previous day had been difficult for the group. They were on a sea kayaking expedition in the Outer Banks of North Carolina as part of an Outdoor Leadership course offered at their university. Part of the curriculum involved having students learn about leadership by taking turns leading the group for a day. Although most of the students in the course were outdoor recreation majors and enjoyed being outdoors, several had had little or no previous experience in sea kayaking.

The students had begun their sea kayaking expedition in good spirits and with a great sense of excitement about finally getting on the water. However, the group soon discovered that the going would be tough as they paddled from the quiet cove near the boat landing around a point into a strong headwind and waves of two to three feet. Before long, the group had become separated. Several paddlers struggled to keep pace with the stronger paddlers, while others struggled to simply keep their boats upright. Despite these challenges, the group forged on, finally ending the day several miles short of the intended destination. As Patrick announced the travel goal for the day, a great sense of trepidation pervaded the group.

Initially, the group made good progress on their second day of paddling. Everyone was paddling well and remained together as a group. Then, suddenly, as they neared the midpoint of a bay, Seth capsized and came out of his kayak. "I don't know if it is my boat or if I just suck!" he sputtered in frustration as his head emerged from the water. He was one of the paddlers who had struggled to remain upright in his boat the previous day, and he had started this day by stating, "I have a personal goal of not flipping over at all today." Chris helped Seth empty his boat and get back in. The group paddled to a beach on the opposite shore of the bay. Everyone got out of their kayaks to stretch and drink some water. Patrick called out to the group, "Bring it in, everyone! Great job paddling across that bay and staying together as a group! We're paddling well enough to keep going. We'll paddle until we find a good lunch spot."

Before continuing, Nate, the course instructor, orchestrated a boat swap among several course participants. It became evident during the crossing of the bay that Seth kept capsizing because the bulkheads in his sea kayak were not water tight. Even though Seth was wearing a spray skirt, his boat was taking on water when he was paddling through the waves. Once water entered the cockpit area of the boat, it drained through the bulkheads into the luggage compartments of his kayak. Consequently, his kayak would gradually fill with water, causing Seth to lose stability and capsize his kayak. To solve the problem, Nate requested that Seth and James exchange kayaks. James had been using a larger kayak that would better accommodate Seth, who happened to be a lineman on the university's football team. And, because James was much smaller than Seth, he would be able to paddle Seth's kayak through the waves without taking on much water. A couple of the other course participants exchanged kayaks as well to resolve a similar problem.

Nate was sorry that he had not realized sooner why Seth and the others had been capsizing so frequently. The group had rented several sea kayaks from a local sea kayaking company, and it turned out that the rental kayaks were not seaworthy. The frequent flips had taken an emotional as well as a physical toll on the group. Bob, who had been paddling one of the rental kayaks and who was even larger than Seth, had proclaimed after one flip, "I hate kayaking and will be happy to never see one again!" After getting underway again, however, it appeared that the boat swap had worked. Everyone remained upright in the kayaks from that point forward.

The group decided to take a break for lunch around noon. Patrick rallied the group: "All right, guys, let's eat some lunch and fill up your water bottles if they are empty." The group had paddled really well together since the earlier break, and Eric was getting excited about the prospect of finally crossing the Sound. "This is great!" he thought. "We are going to make it across the Sound and be on Core Banks tonight!" After lunch, the group began to make way again. As they continued to paddle, however, the wind grew stronger and the waves choppier. Unfortunately, their route was taking them directly into the wind. Sarah discreetly mentioned to James, "I'm getting tired. This wind is as bad as it was yesterday." Taylor struggled to keep up with the group, and the group began to spread out as each member focused on making way against the wind. Patrick finally called out to the group: "Keep paddling and group up behind those sandbags forming that jetty up ahead." This was a good call, because the sandbags created a bit of a windbreak.

Frustration and concern were apparent in the participants' faces. Everyone quickly realized that they were standing on a pile of sandbags littered with trash right next to a harbor filled with fishing boats. Houses lined the shore beyond the fishing boats. Patrick motioned to Eric, the designated navigator for the day, to come help him determine the group's location and how much farther they needed to travel to get to their next campsite. As they studied the charts, Sam pointed in the distance and shouted, "This isn't the island! That's the island!" Patrick realized that a navigational error had been made. "See that island out there?" Patrick said to the group. "We mistook that for the point on the other side of the Sound, and we mistook this point that we are standing on for the island." The plan was to use the island in the distance as a waypoint while crossing the Sound. The participants were disheartened to learn that they had not traveled as far as they had first thought, and that they must paddle four more miles into the wind to reach the planned destination. The entire group was feeling somewhat defeated at this point.

CHARTING A NEW PATH

Nate apologized to Patrick and Eric for giving them some erroneous advice earlier in the day as they were attempting to interpret the charts. He then announced to the group, "All right, gang, I've checked the weather, and twenty- to twenty-five-knot winds are predicted for the next two days. We need to make a decision on how we're going to proceed with this phase of the course." The group would not be able to paddle on open water with winds exceeding fifteen knots, and they were facing the likelihood of being winded-in (i.e., land-bound) for the next couple of days. Patrick asked the group for suggestions.

Eric spoke up first. "I think we should head across the Sound. I think that we can make it." Bob, who was tired and dehydrated, stated, "One option we have is to shuttle back to base camp and try to start over again. We can paddle from Harkers Island to the lighthouse and complete a smaller loop." Pointing to the harbor and the adjacent town, Seth stated, "I wanted to get into the wilderness, and now we are back in civilization." Everyone was tired of paddling against the wind, and multiple participants were reluctant to push on.

Nate, Patrick, and the two assistant instructors broke away from the group to discuss potential options. Meanwhile, Dave and Sam went for a swim. Seth joined them, repeating in a sing-song manner, "This sucks, this sucks, this sucks . . ." Eric stated to Bob, "I really think we can make it. I really want to get to the Outer Banks." Bob was not as optimistic. "I just want to get off this trash pile and away from these houses."

The instructors and Patrick finally returned to the group. Patrick called everyone together and announced to the group that they needed to vote on one of four options that he and the instructors had developed. The first option was to cross Core Sound to the Outer Banks, but, rather than continuing into the wind toward the lighthouse, the group would paddle northward along Cape Lookout National Seashore and eventually return to their starting point near Lola. The second option was based on Bob's suggestion to return to base camp and try to get on the water again the next day with hopes of getting to the lighthouse. The third option was to continue paddling south along the mainland toward the

Harkers Island Ranger Station. The fourth option was to paddle back to Lookout Point, where the group had camped the previous night, and to spend several days exploring that area. They would then finish their trip by returning to the landing near Lola.

Patrick gave the group little time to think about the options before announcing, "This is going to be a secret vote." He quickly explained, "When the option that you want is presented, put your foot into the middle of the circle." Taylor asked, "Can we vote for more than one option?" Chris, one of the assistant instructors, responded, "No. You can only vote for one option." Patrick began the voting process. "All right, everyone circle up and shut your eyes."

"Wow, this is happening way too fast," Eric thought, feeling uncomfortable about the potential ramifications of the decision. After the vote, Patrick announced that the first option—to get off the water, go back to base camp, and reposition the group closer to the lighthouse—had won. Two factions had emerged during the decision-making process, one wanting to continue to paddle and remain in expedition mode even if it meant not making it to the Cape Lookout Lighthouse, and the other wanting to reposition the group with hopes of getting to the lighthouse. One faction split its vote among the three options that involved remaining on the water, while the other faction voted together to get off the water.

It took a lot of effort to implement the decision, and, ultimately, Bob expressed regret that he had even suggested the option. The group paddled back to the harbor where they had eaten lunch earlier. Once back at the harbor, participants pulled the kayaks ashore and unloaded and organized gear while the two assistant instructors hitched a ride to Harkers Island to retrieve the vans and trailers. Once the assistant instructors returned with the vans and trailers, the group loaded all the gear onto the trailers and into the vans and began the drive back to the base camp. There was a lot of tension within the group during the transition, but spirits began to rise as folks began discussing plans for dinner and showers.

AN UNEXPECTED TWIST

As the vans approached the base camp, rather than turning off, they drove right past the campground and continued toward the Harkers Island Ranger Station. "Where are we going? What is going on?" Seth asked. Nate responded, "Just sit tight; we are checking into something else." Once the group arrived at the Harkers Island Ranger Station, Nate informed the passengers in his van, "I need to consult with Chris and Harry, so just hang tight. Patrick, why don't you join us?" As the van doors shut, the van erupted in frustration. Jane exclaimed, "I am so hungry! Why are we not back at camp? I want to start dinner!" Seth added, "I just want to get back to camp so that I can grab a shower and change." Finally, Patrick approached the van. "I need everyone to get out of the van and to circle up." Everyone climbed out of the van wondering what was going on.

Patrick broke the news to the group. "All right, gang, we have a change of plans. We need to get everything out of the trailers and reload the gear into our kayaks. We are going to paddle to an island about a mile from here." The group was silent, but the frustration was palpable. Participants grumbled as they got themselves ready. As Eric and Bob unloaded kayaks from the kayak trailer, Bob whispered, "I am sure glad that we are here and not in the campground." However, it was clear that a number of participants were very upset. As the sun began to set, Nate instructed the group, "Get your headlamps on, and let's get moving."

The group paddled from behind a jetty into a strong headwind on the windward side of the island. Participants paddled frantically at first, worried that they would flip while exiting the small cove behind the jetty and wash into the rip-rap along the shore. However, the group made it onto the Sound without incident and was soon paddling around Shell Point toward the leeward side of Harkers Island. The trip to Browns Island seemed luxurious compared to earlier in the day. The group paddled in calm, following seas with the wind at its back while enjoying the beauty of a sunset over the Sound. The group reached the island just as the sun vanished over the horizon. Everyone set camp, ate dinner, and settled in for the night. Nate came around to check on everyone before bed, informing the participants, "Tomorrow, we will debrief the decision that we made as a group today, and, hopefully, we can work out some of the issues that came up." The next morning, the group woke up to southwesterly winds that were blowing twenty to twenty-five knots. These winds continued for the next two days. Whether the participants liked it or not, they would not be kayaking for the next couple of days.

PROCESSING THE TRIP

After breakfast, everyone gathered in a circle in the sand under some shade trees to debrief the previous day's events. Although the entire group had participated in the decision to get off the water and relocate the group, several members of the group, most notably Nate, the instructor, were not happy with the outcome. Nate opened the discussion by stating to the group, "You made a crux decision to get off the water and to move the group and reconfigure our trip. . . . I feel like we failed in this phase of this course on account of that decision." He then asked each participant to explain why he or she voted as they had the previous day.

Dave explained his motives while also criticizing the instructor team. "I voted number two. . . . I felt like this whole section was an unattainable goal, to make forty miles with a headwind on the Sound. After the first day, I knew the wind wasn't going to change, and it was pretty much just one unattainable goal after another. I am fine with just trying to get to the lighthouse and hanging out on the beach." He also explained that one of his main reasons for voting to change the itinerary was the sense of uncertainty regarding the time and distance left to paddle and the location of the campsite for that evening.

Sarah explained her motives next. "I personally did not vote." She admitted the difficulty she had in making a decision due to being both physically and mentally tired. She also shared Dave's concern about the location of the next campsite. Yet she felt that by choosing option two the group would be "throwing in the towel."

Mark exclaimed, "I voted for number three and all I know is that it was going to keep us on the water!"

Eric said that he ended up voting for what he felt was best for the group. "I actually voted for number two because of the group. I wanted to paddle all day, and I wanted to go all the way across, but it wasn't going to be possible for the group." He explained how frustrating the decision was for him, because he did not want to stop. However, he indicated that the paddle to Browns Island really excited him and that being able to surf the waves and paddle into the sunset was the best part of the trip up to this point.

Bob, who had come up with the option to go back to base camp and start anew, was disappointed with his decision. He described how frustration, fatigue and dehydration had impacted his vote. "I voted for the second option. . . . Sitting on the break for the harbor, looking at the houses, I didn't really feel like we were in a wilderness setting to start with. I was thinking that as long as we are going to be in an area that is mixed with wilderness and nonwilderness, it might be cool to choose another option that would at least give us a chance to see a cultural and historical monument—the lighthouse and all that." He described how in hindsight he would have rather voted for option number four to stay on the water and make a loop of it. He also added that paddling to the island was a great alternative to staying at the base camp. "I mean, that paddle across was definitely one of the highlights of the trip so far. I really enjoyed paddling with the sunset and the challenge of going out into those waves."

Patrick stated, "I didn't vote because I was counting your votes. I didn't even think about how I was going to vote, [though] I probably would have voted for number two." He later confessed to the instructors that he had strongly favored option two and pushed his agenda in the way that he presented the options and conducted the voting process. This was largely because he had been feeling homesick and out of his element camping in a marine environment.

Sam, speaking loudly and energetically, stated, "I want to get to the Atlantic, and I think that is pretty reasonable. . . . I think it should just be the goal! Let's get to the Atlantic! Let's see the ocean!" Sam had a strong desire to get to the lighthouse, and that was one of his major personal goals for this portion of the course. He had voted for option two, because that choice almost guaranteed the opportunity to make it to the lighthouse and to see the Atlantic Ocean.

Ryan said he had voted for option three, because he did not want to leave the field and was disappointed that option two had been chosen. He later stated, "But I am down with whatever decision was made because I am going with the flow." The idea of paddling to Browns Island had angered him the previous evening, but in the end he was glad that they were on the island and not at the campground.

Erin spoke up next and told everyone that she voted for option one because it felt more realistic. She was happy to be on the island and added that her personal goal was related to challenging herself. "This is what I came here for. We are on an expedition. You know it is not supposed to be easy." Erin explained that successfully paddling out from behind the jetty the night before had given her renewed confidence in her kayaking ability.

After all the participants explained their rationales for voting as they did, Nate asked the participants to explain why they were participating in the course. "What I would like to do now is to spend some time talking about goals of the course. Why are we here? I mean, what's this course all about?"

Eric responded, "When I think about goals of the course, I think about them in a couple of different ways. First off, I think about personal goals of the course. . . . And I also think about group goals. . . . And I think one of the frustrating things about that is that they don't always go together, and I think that is one thing that we are missing completely. I don't think that we have all come together as a group yet. I think that we are still kind of out living for ourselves right now." When the group had finished sharing their perspectives on the goals of the course, Nate emphasized the academic goals of the course. "You are getting twelve credits to take part in this course. Why would I bring a class into this setting? Is it about going to see Cape Lookout Lighthouse?" He explained to the group that one of the major goals of the course was to get into expedition mode so that the course goals could be accomplished.

KEY TERMS

communication competence	group member characteristics
conflict	group development
decision making	leadership
group climate	

DISCUSSION QUESTIONS

1. What were the main task and relational issues at stake in this group? How were these issues influenced by differences in group members' goals, skill levels, and experiences?

2. What roles did the various group members (including instructors) assume in this group? How did their roles and behaviors influence the group climate?

3. Why did Nate, the lead instructor, make the decision to change the group plan at the end? Do you think this was an effective and appropriate decision? Why or why not?

4. Was an appropriate leadership style used in this particular situation? Why or why not? How did the leadership style used in this particular situation influence the task/relational balance of this particular group? What would have been the implications of using a different leadership style in this situation?

5. How would you describe the development of this group over the trip? How well do the stage models of group development explain this group's experience?

6. What kind of lessons can we learn from this group that apply to other groups outside of the wilderness expedition context?

BEARS, BOOKS, AND BEER

A Student Group's Attempt at a Public Relations Campaign

Marie D. Montondo and Andrew P. Herman

Four undergraduate students working together on a public relations campaign for class experience conflict as the project progresses.

TUESDAY, FEBRUARY 8, 2 P.M.

Dr. Smith smiled with excitement as she walked into the crowded classroom. She was giving her Introduction to Public Relations class its first major assignment: designing campaigns targeted at their community. One campaign would be implemented as part of an internship with the town board.

"Hello, everybody," she said, "I would like to introduce to you Mr. Rodriguez. As our town supervisor, he is interested in exploring ways the college and town can improve relations. Your job is to design a campaign to meet that goal. Please welcome Mr. Rodriguez as he gives us his vision for this initiative."

Mr. Rodriguez enthusiastically explained some of the constituencies connected to this campaign. Given the stakeholders' varying goals, he offered to provide feedback and information to any student who needed assistance.

SUNDAY, FEBRUARY 21, 10:15 A.M.

"Hey, Taylor, it's Jessica from Public Relations. Not sure where you are, but we're supposed to be meeting in the South Hall computer lab right now. Just get here as soon as you can, okay?"

Taylor swore to herself as she dropped her phone back into her purse. She had completely forgotten about the meeting with her Public Relations work team. "Who schedules a meeting for 10 a.m. on a Sunday, anyway?" she thought to herself as she hurried out of her dorm room.

On her way to South Hall, Taylor tried to recall the purpose of the meeting. They had finally picked a topic for their mock PR campaign a few days ago—maybe today they were working on a logo.

"I'm so sorry, guys," Taylor gushed as she entered the computer lab. Jessica, Lori, and Kym sat clustered around a computer in the corner, looking annoyed.

"Forget about it," said Lori. "Let's just get started."

"What are we working on today?" asked Kym. "Because I e-mailed a friend in the International Students office, and she said she'd be willing to talk to us about making foreign students feel included in the community . . ."

"Wait," interrupted Jessica, "I thought we decided to focus on the student body as a whole and work on students' perceptions of the 'townies.'"

Taylor rolled her eyes. It took the better part of three meetings for the group to come up with a topic, and now they were going to waste yet another meeting arguing about it. "Yes, that is what we agreed on. So let's get to work on the logo."

"I thought we were leaving the logo until next week. It's more important that we get a broad outline of the steps that our campaign will take first," said Jessica.

"Oh, and I've already come up with a few logo ideas," said Lori. "I can pull them up on the computer, if you want."

"Sorry," said Kym, who spoke English as a second language. "What is a logo?"

"It's a sort of symbol," said Taylor, turning to face Kym. "It represents our project, and we put it on all our materials so people recognize the theme of our campaign."

"Here it is!" said Lori proudly.

The other girls gazed at the picture on the screen. It was a picture of a small bear drinking a beer while reading a textbook. Taylor felt her mouth fall open and quickly tried to think of a way to gracefully veto the image. However, Jessica spoke before Taylor could think of an appropriate response.

"Wow, Lori, that's great. It looks just like the bear statue in town. And you did a great job Photoshopping in the beer and book. Everyone will love this!"

While Taylor agreed that Lori's photo editing skills were impressive, she didn't think the school faculty or town officials would approve of a campaign logo taking student alcohol consumption so lightly.

"I don't know, guys," Taylor said. "It looks good, but I'm not sure Dr. Smith will think it's very appropriate."

"What's inappropriate about it?" shot Jessica. "So the bear's drinking a beer. It's perfectly innocent."

"You guys know that underage drinking is a big problem in college towns, and I'm just not sure we should be calling attention to it. Maybe we could change the beer to a slice of pizza. You know, from Mario's Pizzeria in town?" said Taylor.

Jessica ignored her. "Well, I think it's a good attention grabber that could really draw people in to our campaign," she said.

"That's what I thought," said Lori.

"All right, fine. If you guys are sure, we can go with it," Taylor replied. She could see she was going to be overruled, and although she really disliked the logo, she also didn't have the energy to argue about it anymore.

Taylor left the meeting feeling frustrated. While the group had assigned jobs for each member, they had not made any more progress on the logo. Lori and Jessica—members of the same sorority—promised to work on it more. Meanwhile, Taylor would start working on a town walking tour and Kym started a community calendar. Walking back to her dorm, Taylor thought, "I just can't wait for this project to end."

THURSDAY, FEBRUARY 25, 2:00 P.M.

"Hello!" said Dr. Smith, as the students from her PR class strolled into her office. "Is Lori okay?"

"She's finishing chemistry lab so she should be here soon," replied Jessica. "She didn't say anything to me at the sorority house about not being here."

Frustrated, Dr. Smith sat in an empty chair with the group. "When making your appointments, please double-check everybody's calendar so there are no conflicts." Kym and Taylor threw glances at each other—they had said this when they signed up for this time slot.

"Well," continued Dr. Smith, "What have you decided is the focus of your campaign?"

"Relations with the townies!" exclaimed Jessica. "Making international students feel more welcomed," said Taylor simultaneously. Taylor did not like the townie campaign and she wanted to at least let Dr. Smith know that something else had been discussed. After a moment of silence, Jessica turned to Taylor. "I thought we had all agreed on the townie campaign?"

Sensing tension between Jessica and Taylor, Dr. Smith asked the group, "Do you have minutes of your meetings? Or any other kind of record of what you decided?"

Suddenly feeling on the spot, Jessica, Taylor, and Kym nervously shuffled through papers in their folders looking for something to show Dr. Smith. "I guess we don't have anything . . ." said Kym.

"Before you leave today, we need to come to a resolution on your campaign theme," said Dr. Smith.

Just then, Lori entered the office, apologizing for being late. "Perfect timing, Lori—you are here just in time to help make a final decision about your campaign." With a bit of skepticism, Dr. Smith continued, "Why don't you show me what you've learned about how groups make decisions?"

FRIDAY, FEBRUARY 26, 11:30 A.M.

"Okay. Now that we've agreed on the townie campaign, we can finalize our logo," said Jessica.

The girls were gathered around a table in the library's crowded café, their food and papers scattered in front of them. "Lori's got the logo she's been working on. It's not quite finished yet, but it's something to go on," Jessica continued.

Lori nodded, pulled some papers from her folder, and handed out copies. Taylor glanced at the picture. To her disappointment, they had not discussed the beer-drinking bear in their meeting with Dr. Smith. She had hoped the professor would nip the idea in the bud.

"Sorry, why is the bear drinking beer?" asked Kym, furrowing her eyebrows.

"Isn't it cute?" asked Lori.

Jessica hastened to clarify. "It's to explain that the community has more to offer than just bars and college textbook dealers."

"Then shouldn't the bear be doing something other than drinking a beer and reading a textbook?" said Taylor.

"It's ironic. An attention-grabber."

"Well, that's certainly true," thought Taylor, "but definitely not in a good way."

"You're sure that's appropriate?" asked Taylor.

"Oh yeah, the students will respond well to it," said Lori.

Taylor saw she was not going to win this one. She glanced at Kym and shrugged, then looked back at Jessica. "Well, if you're sure . . . "

"Good," said Jessica. "Since we are all in agreement and Lori's been doing such good work, I think we should let her continue on the logo. Once that's finished we can add it to the brochures I'm working on. Um, that leaves . . ."

"My tour," interrupted Taylor, who had designed a walking tour of the town for new students. "I found some cool historical locations and typed up descriptions, if you want to see them." She pulled a few sheets out of a folder. "Kym and I are going to take photos of them to add to the campaign materials."

"Great." Lori glanced at the descriptions. "That just leaves the events calendar." She looked at Kym.

Kym looked taken aback. It was clear she had not understood that she was supposed to have started the calendar.

"She's made some great contacts," Taylor intervened. "And I sent her a list of events I found on the town board's website."

Kym gave Taylor a grateful smile. "So now I put those events in our calendar and bring it to class."

"We're all set for today?" asked Lori. "Because I have another meeting."

Jessica nodded and she and Lori packed away their papers. As much as Taylor disliked these meetings, she felt Jessica and Lori were ending this one hastily.

"Are you sure we're ready for our next meeting with Dr. Smith? I don't feel like we made a great impression last time."

"Oh, I'm sure we'll be fine," said Jessica. "See you guys Wednesday?"

WEDNESDAY, MARCH 3, 10:00 A.M.

"Hi, everyone. Good to see you again," said Dr. Smith as she welcomed the group into her office. "How is the campaign looking?"

"Great!" replied Lori excitedly. "You're really going to like the materials we put together. The campaign's all mapped out—a cool logo and tagline, a fun walking tour for new students, and a calendar of events so students know what's going on during the school year." It suddenly dawned on Lori that she was not really sure if Kym had finished the calendar since the group had not communicated since their last meeting.

"That sounds productive! Since the logo is the most pressing issue right now, why don't we look at that?" suggested Dr. Smith.

Opening her folder, Lori pulled out her most recent version of the logo. She had put a lot of work into the drawing and hoped Dr. Smith noticed. "I really captured the likeness of the bear statue from Main Street," thought Lori, "and that glass of beer sure looks realistic."

Taking the drawing from Lori, Dr. Smith could feel her frustration rising as different thoughts went through her head. "Aren't these guys aware of the tensions—both on campus and with the town—surrounding the issue of students drinking?"

As the professor, Dr. Smith had the authority to veto aspects of students' projects. However, she was not the actual client, so she hesitated to use this power. She always considered how any intervention would impact the learning experience each group had with the client. Sometimes, it was good for a group to experience the response to a poorly thought-out campaign. She quickly thought, "Should I veto the logo now or let the group see how people respond during the presentations?"

She decided to withhold her feelings for now. "So . . . talk to me about your logo."

Jessica jumped in. "We wanted to show students that the town is more than bars and bookstores."

"And so the bear is drinking a beer because . . . " interrupted Dr. Smith.

"It's like an ironic situation that will catch someone's attention. You'll see the bear drinking a beer, but then we'll tell you about all the other neat things you can do in town."

"I see . . . "

"Excuse me," said Kym, cutting in, "but could someone tell me what 'ironic' means?"

"It's when something doesn't mean exactly what you think it should mean," replied Jessica, a bit testily. 我听不懂

"You have clearly put a lot of effort into your materials so far," noted Dr. Smith. "But I do have some questions for you to discuss at your next meeting. Now, as we discussed in class, there are multiple publics to consider when constructing a campaign. Have you discussed your potential publics? A campaign exists in historical and current contexts. How might the students and residents respond to a beer-drinking bear? What other issues might you need to think about?"

Taylor shot an annoyed look at Jessica and Lori. These were some of the very points she had made in their discussions. Student drinking was a problem—or at least was perceived as a problem—in the town. Mixing beer with the town's iconic bear was likely to set off alarms, even with some of the students. "Why don't these two get that?" thought Taylor, annoyed.

The meeting ended with Dr. Smith reminding the group of a few items they should think about in preparation for the upcoming presentation. After the group left, Dr. Smith continued to question whether she should have been more forceful about the logo.

SATURDAY, MARCH 13, 2:00 P.M.

"Okay, guys, there are only a few days left until our presentation, so we need to finish everything up ASAP," said Jessica, beginning the meeting. "Lori's volunteered to put together a PowerPoint, so now we just need to divide up sections for us each to present."

The team was gathered for their final meeting in an empty classroom. With the presentation in three days, Taylor was relieved she would not have to deal with this dysfunctional workgroup anymore, but also nervous about the audience response to their presentation.

"Yeah, yeah, sounds good," said Taylor. "Listen, have you given any more thought to changing the logo? Dr. Smith really seemed to dislike it."

"We only have three days until it's due; it's too late," said Jessica.

"Besides, the students will love it," added Lori, "and their opinions count toward our grade."

"It's fine," said Jessica with finality. "Now, Kym, since your events calendar could make a good first point in our presentation, would you give the introduction as well?"

A few hours later the meeting ended. After Jessica cut off the logo discussion, Taylor and Kym shut down and simply agreed to Lori and Jessica's ideas. The group muddled through the outline of the presentation and Lori promised to get the slides done before Monday. Since everybody had conflicting schedules before Tuesday's presentation, they ended up meeting at 11 p.m. Monday, which worried Kym because she had an 8 a.m. biology lab on Tuesday.

Taylor walked home with a mixture of emotions about the last few weeks of the group's meetings. "What went wrong with our group? How could we develop such a disastrous PR campaign? How come we communicated so poorly when we are supposed to know better?"

TUESDAY, MARCH 16, 3:22 P.M.

There is a buzz of nervous excitement in the room as students enter and make last-minute changes to their presentations. Dr. Smith is already there, chatting in the back with Mr. Rodriguez and two other town administrators.

Kym, Jessica, and Lori huddle together, flipping through the PowerPoint slides one last time. Kym is anxious that her English is not strong enough to do the introduction. All three of them are on edge because Taylor has not shown up yet.

"Why am I not surprised that she's the one who's late?" remarks Jessica.

"Because she always is," mutters Lori.

At that moment, Taylor rushes in, breathless.

"Sorry," says Taylor. "Some guy who likes to hear himself talk would not shut up in my last class and we went late."

"It's fine," responds Lori, raising her eyebrows at Jessica. "We're scheduled to go later in class."

Five groups later, Lori, Jessica, Kym, and Taylor stand up to begin the presentation. Although she's nervous, Kym's introduction and presentation of the calendar goes well. Taylor shows some great pictures of the town to support her idea of a walking tour. Jessica enhances her brochure discussion with useful information about the community. They save the logo until the end of the presentation to reinforce their point that the town offers students more than bars and bookstores.

Lori puts up the logo slide and begins to talk. Taylor, Kym, and Jessica see some of the students snickering. Taylor thinks others look confused. The town administrators are not laughing. Instead, some raise their eyebrows as they glance at each other. Lori doesn't notice. After the presentation, the group members sit down with very different perceptions of how it has gone.

At the end of the class, Mr. Rodriguez gets up to speak. "I always enjoy coming to Dr. Smith's class to see the creative and insightful ideas in many of these presentations. I would like to thank Dr. Smith for inviting us to hear your ideas. We took notes during your presentations and received your formal proposals. We will review these and, with Dr. Smith, choose one for further development. I would like to thank all of you for the thoughtful effort each of your proposals represents."

AFTER THE PRESENTATION

In written feedback from Dr. Smith, the group learned that while some portions of their proposal were strong, their campaign was not chosen because of the logo: "While some people may see the beer as harmless, the town administrators expressed concern that the issue of underage drinking was taken so lightly in a campaign to improve town-gown relations. I hope your group will take this as a learning experience about the importance of careful consideration when choosing materials for publication in a campaign."

Jessica and Lori were not happy—they felt that the rest of the class had responded well during the presentation. Taylor was not surprised—though she was a bit sad that her walking tour idea was not picked up. Mostly, she was glad the project was done. Kym was frustrated. She was not used to so much tension in a group. She had also hoped for a better grade to help pull her GPA up. And Dr. Smith still wondered if she should have intervened.

KEY TERMS

conflict	group outcomes
cultural norms	interdependence
decision making	roles
diversity	

DISCUSSION QUESTIONS

1.   What went wrong with this group's communication? Why do you think each group member had such a different perspective on the quality of their product and presentation?

2.   What roles and norms developed in this group? How did these norms and roles influence the group outcomes?

3.   As an international student, Kym is struggling to be a part of this group. Which cultural orientations are influencing the communication between Kym and the rest of the group members? What should the group do to benefit from these different orientations and make Kym's experience more productive and pleasant?

4. As a group, the four students are faced with a number of conflict situations. Identify the dominant conflict style of each member of the group and support your choice with an example from the case. How does each person's conflict style influence the outcome of the group?

5. To what extent did people outside of the group influence the group process and outcome? What could the group have done differently to better account for the external stakeholders like the community leaders who were judging the presentations?

ON WHAT BASIS DO YOU CONCLUDE THAT I AM A RACIST?

Robert Whitbred

A student group's struggle with time management, goal setting, collaboration, and equality ends in a major conflict.

"On what basis could you possibly conclude that I am a racist? You honestly need to get over yourself and quit being such an idiot," Greg yelled.

Renee exclaimed in a loud voice, "I have been putting up with your crap for weeks now, and all you do is stomp around and make accusations based on nothing but your fantasies."

"The fact is that you all have been working on this project for a month without me. You dropped the part I liked and have left me out of everything. If it is not because of my skin color, then what is it?" Patricia responded. At this point, the professor who had called the meeting stepped in and took over the conversation.

DIVERSITY OF GROUP MEMBERS AND EMERGENT NORMS

Dave, Matt, Patricia, Renee, and Greg were members of a team charged with completing a research project over the four months of an academic term. Dave was a white single man in his mid-twenties. He was attending college part time while working full time. Matt was a married white man in his early thirties. He was was going to college full time and working part time. Patricia was a married black woman in her mid-thirties with two kids. Patricia was going to college full time but was not working. Greg, a single white man, and Renee, a single half Arabic and half white woman, were both twenty years old and "traditional" full-time college students without jobs.

At their first meeting during class time in the second week of the term, Greg stated, "Take a look at this assignment—it says we are supposed to find journal articles and write hypotheses, collect and analyze data, and write a paper. This is impossible."

Renee took a look at the assignment and added, "These instructors think we have nothing else to do, and that their class is the only important class."

"And to make it even better, this is the most useless junk we're ever going to have to deal with," Dave chimed in.

At this point, Matt said, "I guess we should start to figure out how we are going to do this."

"What about a study that looks at whether there are differences in the communication styles for males and females and blacks and whites? This was covered in two of my other classes, and I filled out a communication styles survey thing last week. I think this would be easy to do. What do you think?" Patricia asked.

Without much time for thought Renee responded, "That sounds fine to me. What do you all think?" As the discussion continued each member of the group agreed to the project. They also made plans to spend the next week finding journal articles. Dave, Renee, and Greg would focus on gender. Matt and Patricia would look for materials on ethnicity. The meeting concluded with members comparing schedules and setting up regular meetings to take place every Wednesday at 9 a.m. in the lobby of the Communication Department.

The following Wednesday, Dave, Renee, and Greg showed up for the meeting on time, while Matt arrived fifteen minutes late. He offered a token apology, saying, "I'm sorry—I got hung up late last night and overslept." The others did not respond.

After another fifteen minutes passed, Greg said, "I don't think Patricia is going to show up, and I don't see how we are going to do anything without her. We should bag this until next week." The others agreed and left the lobby. At 9:45, Patricia arrived at the meeting place to find no one there. She immediately called Dave and asked, "Where are you? I was late because I had to drop my son off at day care."

"We waited for a long time, and when you did not show up, we decided to cancel the meeting. We'll meet next week," Dave replied.

At the following week's meeting, only Dave and Renee arrived on time. Matt and Patricia were fifteen minutes late. This time, Dave asked, "Why am I sitting here so early when not everyone is here? We cannot do anything on a group project unless all of us are here. I guess we'll have to pick this up next week. I'm going back to bed."

Patricia then said, "We are now three weeks into the course, and we have essentially done nothing. I'm getting worried about this."

"As one of the only ones who has been here all the time and on time, I'm getting tired of others not showing up on time, and then hearing those same people complain. I'm not wasting time when we're not all here," Renee responded. With that, the meeting adjourned.

The next week, all five members arrived at nine, but Dave announced, "I need to leave in twenty minutes. My car broke, and my mother is picking me up to drop me off at work by eleven. If I don't leave then, I will not be able to get to work."

In response to Dave's announcement, the four other members expressed their collective frustration. Group members accused one another of being irresponsible, unreliable, and unreasonable. Finally, Greg suggested, "I think it is obvious we cannot all meet together at this or any other time. We need to communicate through e-mail. Otherwise, we're not going to get any of this done. We can talk in person before and after class, but otherwise we'll need to do this electronically." Everyone exchanged e-mail addresses and phone numbers, and then left the meeting.

COMPUTER-MEDIATED COMMUNICATION, ACCUSATIONS, AND CONFLICT

Two days later, Greg sent out the following e-mail:

> From: Greg
>
> To: Dave, Renee, Patricia, Matt
>
> Subject: Sex and Comm
>
> I went to the library yesterday, and found a bunch of stuff on sex and communication styles. I got about ten articles. Has anyone else gotten anything?

Renee responded:

> From: Renee
>
> To: Dave, Patricia, Matt, Greg
>
> Subject: Sex and Comm
>
> What an overachiever—I have not done anything yet. In all seriousness, I'll get to this over the weekend.

Dave quickly added:

> From: Dave
>
> To: Renee, Patricia, Matt, Greg
>
> Subject: Sex and Comm
>
> I've been able to find about four things, but not as many as you. I'll bring them to the next class.

Matt simply replied:

> From: Matt
>
> To: Renee, Patricia, Dave, Greg
>
> Subject: Sex and Comm
>
> I've been swamped at work. I'll get to this over the weekend sometime.

Greg then sent out a final message to everyone:

> From: Greg
>
> To: Renee, Patricia, Dave, Matt
>
> Subject: Concern
>
> I know we are all busy and have a bunch of stuff going on, but we need to be sure we get moving on this project. Let's talk and compare things before class next week.

Dave, Matt, Renee, and Greg talked briefly before the next class. Patricia was not in class, but she had called Dave that morning noting that she needed to take care of her ill child. The group agreed to continue to coordinate the project via e-mail. Later that day, Renee sent out the following e-mail:

> From: Renee
>
> To: Dave, Greg
>
> Subject: Articles
>
> I just got finished with some keyword searches of that CommAbstracts database and dug up four articles. What have the rest of you found? I know Greg has a bunch of stuff.

Dave hit Reply:

> From: Dave
>
> To: Renee, Greg
>
> Subject: Articles
>
> I have five journal articles that directly relate to what we are doing. I think we have enough on gender. Do we have anything on race?

Greg noticed that Renee had not included Matt or Patricia on her mailing list and sent an e-mail to all five members:

> From: Greg
>
> To: Dave, Renee, Patricia, Matt
>
> Subject: Project
>
> Hi all. Renee, Dave, and I have found quite a bit of useful material on the gender/sex to communication styles part. What do we have so far on race?

Matt replied:

> From: Matt
>
> To: Dave, Renee, Patricia, Greg
>
> Subject: Project
>
> I'm sorry about this, but I've been getting creamed at both work and home. I know this is no excuse, but I have not had any time. Has anyone heard from or seen Patricia?

Greg then proposed:

> From: Greg
> To: Dave, Renee, Patricia, Matt
> Subject: Project
>
> Why don't we drop the race thing and focus on gender? We have what we need, and there is plenty here.

Matt responded:

> From: Matt
> To: Dave, Renee, Patricia, Greg
> Subject: Project
>
> It is fine with me. Do you think this will be okay with Patricia?

Frustrated, Greg read Matt's message and stated:

> From: Greg
> To: Dave, Renee, Matt
> Subject: Project
>
> I do not mean to be harsh, but I really don't care what she has to say. We can never find her anyway.

Later that day, the instructor of the class sent out the following e-mail:

> From: Instructor
> To: Methods Class
> Subject: Project Update
>
> Hi, everyone. We are now seven weeks into the term, and I have not heard from some of you. This is not a necessarily a problem, but I am concerned that progress may not be being made. Please either send me a detailed e-mail updating me on your progress or schedule a meeting with me to talk.

Greg responded with an e-mail to both the instructor and the rest of the group:

> From: Greg
> To: Instructor, Dave, Renee, Patricia, Matt
> Subject: Project Update
>
> Hi. We apologize that our group has not met with you yet, but we have been working hard. We have found a lot of journal articles and are almost done with the first parts of the paper. We should be ready to meet with you soon and are ready to begin data collection at your earliest convenience. By the way—we got a lot of research on gender and essentially noth-

ing on race. Thus, we decided to drop the stuff that has to do with race, since we don't think it's necessary to do both.

A flurry of e-mails were sent between the group members from 10 p.m. to 3 a.m. that evening. These were also cc'd to the instructor. The first was from Patricia:

From: Patricia

To: Greg, Dave, Renee, Matt

CC: Instructor

Subject: Project?

I'm confused and a bit upset. I don't believe that you have done so much on this project without getting my input. How could you write so much without me? I also find it very suspicious that as the only African American woman in the group, I was the one that was blown off and excluded. You also decided without me to drop the variable I was most interested in—which is not coincidently race.

Renee responded:

From: Renee

To: Patricia, Greg, Dave, Matt

CC: Instructor

Subject: Project?

Who the @#$% do you think you are accusing me of this? I am half Arabic. I am also well aware of biases and stereotypes, and do not appreciate being accused of this. You need to take a powder and relax!

Greg said:

From: Greg

To: Renee, Patricia, Dave, Matt

CC: Instructor

Subject: Project?

Patricia, I'm sorry that you are upset, but you need to understand that we have not seen or heard from you for weeks. When you do show up, you are late and take off right after class is over. We have not received any e-mails from you, and you have not provided us with any material about race. I'm sorry we made the decision without you, but we had to move forward.

Matt jumped into the conversation:

From: Matt

To: Renee, Patricia, Greg, Dave

CC: Instructor

Subject: Project?

You are such an idiot. At least I admit that I dropped the ball on this one and left it up to the others on the team to do something. You are obviously not mature enough to admit this. Instead, you lob insults at everyone and blame us for your disappearing act.

Patricia replied:

From: Patricia
To: Renee, Matt, Greg, Dave
CC: Instructor
Subject: Project?

Now I'm being accused of being immature on top of everything else. For your information, I have collected a bunch of stuff, but now I find out that you have been writing the paper without me. Someone explain to me how in a group that has three white males, a white female, and a black woman, it is only the black woman who has been left out. I'm sorry, but this is ridiculous and unacceptable, and I'm going to see the professor.

In response to Patricia's message, Dave asked:

From: Dave
To: Renee, Matt, Greg, Patricia
CC: Instructor
Subject: Project?

What are you going to see him (the professor) about?

Patricia responded:

From: Patricia
To: Renee, Matt, Greg, Dave
CC: Instructor
Subject: Project?

To start with, I'll talk about the inappropriate and unfair way I have been treated.

Upset by the unfolding accusations, Renee stated:

From: Renee
To: Patricia, Matt, Greg, Dave
CC: Instructor
Subject: Project?

Go ahead and do whatever you want to. I'm going to see the professor and get you dropped from the group. The problem here is that you have not done anything. Now the bigger problem is you making insane, yes, insane accusations. Get a life.

Case 15 | *On What Basis Do You Conclude That I Am a Racist?*   **121**

The instructor, having now read all of this, interjected:

From: Instructor

To: Renee, Patricia, Matt, Greg, Dave

CC: Instructor

Subject: Project?

This has gotten out of hand. I strongly suggest that none of you send any more e-mails or have any further communication with one another until we can meet. I am free for an hour after class today. I very strongly suggest that we all meet, and that you reschedule any other commitments you may have in that hour following class.

The meeting after class was not pleasant. The instructor began, "I've got to admit that this is the first time in my experience that a group project has gotten this personal. I've never seen things go so wrong without my being aware of the problems. Why don't we start with each of you describing what happened?"

Patricia pushed forward. "To put it bluntly, they are racist and biased against the material I want to include. They dropped race from the paper and wrote a bunch of the things without including me in any discussions." At this point, Greg interrupted and the dialogue this case opened with ensued.

KEY TERMS

conflict

computer-mediated communication

diversity

feedback

group climate

roles

task and relational communication

DISCUSSION QUESTIONS

1. Describe how diversity was present in this group. What are the ways in which group members differed from each other? How does diversity influence groups?

2. What norms were developed in this group related to time and accountability of group members? How did these norms develop? How can other groups avoid developing these norms?

3. At one point the group switched to using e-mail to communicate with each other. How does communication via e-mail differ from face-to-face communication?

4. How was email communication effectively used to help the project move forward? How did email communication contribute to the conflict and accusations that occurred?

5. What were the substantive issues involved in this conflict? How does group member diversity influence how members view these substantive issues?

6. What caused the conflict to become personal? How could this have been avoided?

7. If you were the professor, what would you have the group do next?

 **PART** *Problem Solving and Decision Making*

Matters of Life and Death

Decision-Making in a Jury

Mridula Mascarenhas, Renee A. Meyers, and Joseph A. Bonito

A jury struggles to come to a consensus in a murder trial.

In 2004, ABC News filmed a jury as they made decisions in a capital murder case. This was a historic moment because cameras are seldom allowed into a jury room. The defendant (name changed to Matthew Dawson), a 47-year-old white male, was charged with committing two murders. The first victim was his common-law wife (a drug abuser). The second victim was Matthew's friend, a drug addict. Matthew, who was unemployed, lived with his mother and had a history of both dealing and using illegal drugs.

The key evidence against Matthew in the trial was provided by a paid police informant with prior convictions and a drug habit. This informant befriended Matthew after the two deaths and, wearing a wire, recorded Matthew claiming that he had already used drug cocktails to kill two people and would be willing to do it again for a price. Matthew's defense attorney argued that Matthew was indeed a drug addict, but that he was also a compulsive liar who had bragged about these two killings only to impress others, and that he had not actually murdered anyone.

There were twelve jurors. After several days, the jurors convicted Matthew of the two murders. Then the jury had to decide on a sentence for Matthew and had four choices: (1) death penalty, (2) life with the possibility of parole after twenty-five years, (3) life with the possibility of parole after thirty years, or (4) life without the possibility of parole. When the first vote was taken early in the discussion, half the jurors were ready to send Matthew to his death. As the discussion progressed, some jurors argued that he should be given one of the other life sentences.

Jurors had to be unanimous. If one juror disagreed with any of the sentence choices, the judge would not impose it. If the jurors could not unanimously agree on a single choice, they were required to declare themselves a hung jury, and the judge would impose the sentence she thought most appropriate.

We tell the story of this jury deliberation from Juror #4's point of view. This narrative is fictional but it is grounded in the actual jury transcripts.[1] The names of the defendant and jurors have been changed, and the division of the deliberations into three days is also fictional. Jurors' statements reflect the flow and tenor of the original discussion but are not necessarily their exact wording.

STATE OF OHIO VS. MATTHEW DAWSON: THE EXPERIENCE OF JUROR #4

I don't like picturing that jury room. Instantly, I feel the knot in my stomach and that dull headache again. It's not easy knowing that a man's fate hinges on a single decision you make. Who thinks they'd ever have that kind of power? I don't know if the other jurors were any better prepared for this experience than me. In looking back, I'd say we all tried to do what we thought was right. Maybe it was easier for some than for others. I don't really regret the outcome. But I do wonder sometimes about what we said, what we could have said, and how, in the end, it might have been different.

Maybe it's best if I start with a few introductions. You need to know Steve Wheeler, Juror #1. He was elected as the jury foreman. Personally I think he did well in this role, but I know some of the jurors didn't like him. They didn't care for his deliberate, slow-paced style. I think we needed some of that, though, to take the edge off the tensions between us. You'll also need to know about Cynthia Jansen, Juror #12. She's the one you're most likely to have heard about. The news reports called her "the lone holdout." They said she's the reason we ended up as we did. To an extent, that's true. But I don't think Cynthia alone was responsible for our outcome. I have to mention Pamela Clarke next. She was Juror #7. She was sort of a nemesis—Cynthia's nemesis because they were opponents throughout, but also Nemesis, like the Greek goddess of retribution. Pamela was convinced about Dawson's guilt and she wanted the death penalty. She didn't want to give him life when he'd taken it away from two other people.

Those were the key jurors. The rest of us were less vocal or at least we weren't vocal all the time. Some of the other juror names you'll hear are Rick, Gabe, Carl, Pat, and Doris. We'd all heard the same facts. But you know how it is. Two people hear the same thing and they

---

[1]More information about the case can be found in:

Francis, T. (2004, August 11). Juror's burden. *Cleveland Scene*. Retrieved from http://www.clevescene.com/cleveland/jurors-burden/Content?oid=1487421

Ohio vs. Ducic: Injustice Files—Lee Fleming blog post. Retrieved from http://www.leefleming.com/neurotwitch/index.php?/weblog/comments/ohio_v_ducic_injustice_files/ on March 25, 2010

State v. Ducic, 162 Ohio App.3d 721, 2005-Ohio-4291. Retrieved from http://www.sconet.state.oh.us/rod/docs/pdf/8/2005/2005-ohio-4291.pdf on March 25, 2010

Sunwolf (in press). Investigating jury deliberation in a capital murder case. *Small Group Research*.

don't agree on what it means. That's the good part about having twelve people decide. We helped each other remember what was said and what was left out in that courtroom. Often, we argued over the meaning of the instructions we were given. That's where I'd like to start, with our first big discussion about "mitigating factors."

DAY 1

The first evening's deliberations were about balancing the aggravating and the mitigating factors in the case, in order to decide on death or one of the possible life sentences. We didn't really understand what mitigating factors were and we all had different opinions about what counted. As we started to argue, it became clear that we weren't even defining the concept the same way. It frustrated me that most of the jurors wouldn't address this basic discrepancy. We could argue till the cows came home but we needed to realize that we weren't even starting from the same place. I began to tune out, when Steve finally addressed the issue. Although he was naturally soft-spoken, he raised his voice to get our attention. "We were discussing something that I'd like to dwell on for a minute. It has to do with mitigating factors, okay? They are factors that lessen the moral culpability of the defendant. I think a good example would be if a lifelong alcoholic quit alcohol and went to AA."

Rick shot back in disagreement. I had a feeling Rick was a little resentful of Steve. Rick seemed like one of those busy banker guys. He was always impeccably dressed and checking his BlackBerry anytime he could. He insisted, "I think mitigating is different from what you think. I mean, a mitigating factor is that he can't stop taking the drug, not that he goes to AA." Then Cynthia made a pretty wise observation. She said we had to find a better way to define the word "mitigating." That gave Gabe the idea to call for a dictionary. Somebody laughed at Gabe's suggestion. I never thought that we'd need a dictionary in that jury room either, but at that moment, it seemed like a good idea to get out of our own minds and look to something objective for a change. Someone brought us a pretty tattered dictionary, and Rick read out that mitigating meant "to make something less harsh." I volunteered that Dawson's drug abuse and his depression counted as mitigating factors. But Steve argued that he couldn't see how drug abuse fit. Little side conversations started at this point, and Steve tried to call us to attention again.

Then Gabe stepped in. "I think to find mitigating factors, we need to look for the good side to Dawson, which could cancel out some of the bad. I believe Dawson was all along sending out cries for help and that his pathological lying and his bravado and all that they were really just cries for attention." I saw Pamela rolling her eyes while Gabe talked, but he was sitting two seats away, so he didn't notice. Cynthia started off even before Gabe finished. "I just want to remind everyone about all those places on the tape where Dawson had talked about doing things around the house, cutting the grass and just living like a normal person, you know." She and Gabe seemed to have developed a tag team, because he picked up right after her and went on about how Dawson was constantly putting himself down by calling himself a druggie, and a loser, and how it's hard to deal with an addiction. Then he started to tell us about trying to quit smoking himself and how if someone would take away his cigarettes, he'd get in a foul mood, and so he understood Dawson's emotional battle with addiction. Pamela interrupted to ask if his mood got so foul that he'd kill someone in that state. Pamela had a way with her sarcastic one-liners. They usually made me laugh, but they didn't make me like her any better. I was never sure when one of those would be launched at me.

Steve thought this was a good place to diffuse some of the tension, so he suggested we vote for or against the death penalty. It turned out to be an even split. We sat there looking at each other for a few seconds, and then Cynthia spoke up. She seemed both scared and determined, "I want him to have twenty-five years. I have hope." Doris, who reminded me a lot of an aunt of mine and who usually didn't speak up unless she had something significant to say, asked Cynthia, "You have hope that what?" Cynthia explained, "Maybe with him having a religious background, you know he might find Jesus while he's in prison." Then Doris said the most unexpected thing, at least in terms of the religious stereotype I had of her. She said, "He could be in prison a lifetime serving the Lord. He doesn't have to be outside serving Jesus."

As frustrated as I was starting to become with Cynthia, I couldn't deny that she was earnest. I think she completely meant it when she said she hoped Dawson would find Jesus in prison. Doris's comment cracked us up, though, and several of us tried to stifle the laughter. Cynthia didn't seem upset, I think she even smiled a little, but it was a sad sort of smile. It occurred to me then that we weren't just bringing our minds into that jury room; we were laying our personalities, our beliefs, our feelings on the line. And Dawson wasn't the only person being judged.

We continued to deliberate about mitigating circumstances and sentencing options for a while. I felt that we never really got it right. We kept reading the instructions they gave us and the dictionary definition, and they both said a mitigating circumstance is something that lessens the moral culpability of the convicted person. I think we all understood that, yet we disagreed on how to apply it to the sentencing. Some of the jurors wanted to consider Dawson's drug addiction as a mitigating factor, but others didn't think he should get credit for abusing drugs. We talked past each other without making headway. Finally, realizing we weren't getting anywhere, the foreman decided we should adjourn. I was glad to call it a night.

DAY 2

I voted against the death penalty yesterday, and I was leaning toward thirty years. Cynthia wanted to give Dawson only twenty-five, and that didn't seem like enough justice to others. This was the day it became clear that Pamela and Cynthia were in opposite camps. They were both equally passionate about their positions. Cynthia stood up for Dawson as often as she could. This was a man we had all (including her) convicted of murder. But she still felt sympathy for him. I didn't like sentencing Dawson any more than she did, but I did realize we were charged with following the law, and sometimes the law requires you to do something you may not feel happy about. I remember Steve's opening comment that day. He sounded hopeful and positive—maybe he'd gotten a better night's sleep than I had. I remember he said that it was a very important day and that we had to find our way to the same page and deliver justice. That word "deliver" stuck in my mind. It sounded so easy, as if all we had to do was wrap justice in a package and deliver it to the judge. It turned out to be a tough discussion. I will try to reproduce for you a key part of the deliberations.

Carl: I'll go with thirty. My first choice is life without parole. I think he needs to live a long time thinking about what he did.

Pamela: Dawson took the right of life away from two people. It's our duty to take his rights away from him. The correct thing to do is to give him exactly what he gave them—death— but the humane thing to do is life without parole. I will not do thirty.

Pat: If you give him twenty-five, he might have a second chance when he gets out.

Cynthia: You are thinking it's all emotion, but it's not, it's testimony. The doctor talked about his drugs and depression.

Pamela: That's not evidence.

Cynthia: These are all evidence. We heard these things in court. And I'd like to add that we heard too, he was an altar boy.

Pamela: That's irrelevant.

Cynthia: No, that's testimony. Did the state prove Matthew deserves to die or spend the rest of his life in jail? I don't think so. Did the defense do the best job for him? No, I don't think so.

Steve: Whether you like it or not, you took an oath to uphold the law. I want you to tell me how twenty-five years is justice?

(Cynthia hesitated a while before her response. I even think her voice sounded a little choked.)

Cynthia: I have to be true to myself and to the oath. This doesn't deserve death.

Steve: Explain to me how I can give Dawson only twenty-five years. I can't give his victims the same option.

Carl: I don't want to say anything against those victims because I didn't know them, but they did do drugs. They were drug addicts too.

Cynthia: The law doesn't tell us what to think. It tells us to weigh factors. You have to interpret the law to understand the law.

Steve: Okay, let's make a list of mitigating factors. First I am going to put down he was an altar boy.

Rick: I know a million Catholic boys who were altar boys and then turned into juvenile delinquents.

Steve: So you wouldn't give it much weight.

Rick: No, I wouldn't.

Cynthia: I would weigh it as showing there is a possibility of good behavior.

Pamela: Yesterday, after thinking about this for a while, I felt the drug addiction played a part, but then I thought, that's really irrational to say that it's okay to commit a crime if you're high. An addiction is by choice, it's by choice.

Rick (looking at Cynthia): And it was said that he wasn't drugged up all the time. How do you know? He could have planned to kill those two when he was completely sober. We have to weigh the aggravating circumstances against the mitigating circumstances.

Steve: But the problem is not mathematics. You can't attach numbers to these things. Killing two people, in my opinion, is insurmountable weight. To me, murder versus anything miti-gating, it doesn't balance out.

I think the foreman's observation summed up our collective difficulty. We felt that we were playing a game of life and death, trying to make the mitigating circumstances cancel out the aggravating circumstances, or vice versa. But it wasn't an ordinary game. We were weighing the lives of Dawson's victims against his own. How do you come out on the right side of that equation?

DAY 3

This was the hardest day of all. We felt the pressure to arrive at our judgment, but we were tired of going around in circles. It was becoming clear that certain jurors were intractable; they were going to stick to their positions. I believe they had their rea-sons. It makes you wonder what you can say or do in a jury room that would change people's minds, if they've already made them up one way or another. I think what struck me most on this last day was the incredible challenge that a juror has, to decide among three things—what's fair by the law, what can be unanimously agreed on, and what feels right by one's personal conscience. If those three don't line up, it can be hell, personally and in terms of the jury's deliberations. I realized too, how much we rely on personal experience and personal opinion in making decisions, even though we're supposed to be applying the law only to the facts we heard in the courtroom. When you're deciding the fate of a fellow human being, how do you put your own hu-manity aside?

We were all starting to get exhausted. Steve seemed to look more worn out with every passing hour. Finally, he said in a firm voice to no one in particular, although I had a feeling he was addressing Cynthia, "We do have the murder of two people, do you agree with that? Murder, which I believe is one of the Ten Commandments. What weight do you give murdering two people, and how do you equate that to the sum of the mitigating factors?" Rick turned in Cynthia's direction and asked, "Can you tell me a crime that has more weight than mass murder?" All of us looked at Cynthia and I felt a mixture of irritation and sympathy for her. I think the rest of us understood that we had a sense of duty to each other and to the law. I don't know if Cynthia understood that, or if she did, maybe it didn't matter as much to her.

Steve suggested a vote, but then he voiced the fear that had been gathering in all of us for some time. He told us we needed to think about our vote carefully because we were on the verge of a hung jury. We weren't going to get anywhere unless some of us were willing to budge. But Pamela made her position clear. "I am intractable. Life without parole, that's where I am willing to go." Steve said he didn't want to change his position, but he was willing to go from life to thirty for the sake of a compromise. Pamela retorted that he shouldn't have to do anything he didn't want to.

I was willing to compromise too if we could reach an agreement. I think I was relieved when we didn't select the death penalty. Beyond that, I felt Dawson deserved some time in jail; if it was life or thirty, or maybe even twenty-five, I was okay with it. Then Steve asked Cynthia, since we all knew she was the one who would hold out on the other end, "Okay, Cynthia, I'm going to ask you, are you intractable on thirty years, you won't move to life?" This time Cynthia didn't hesitate; she looked directly at Steve and then around the room and she shook her head as she said, "I can't do life." Pamela pushed her seat away in frustration and told Steve it was time for him to write up the note for the judge. She wasn't the only one upset with Cynthia. Rick confronted her. "Say that he comes out of jail after thirty years and does it again, how would you feel? Would you still feel you made the right decision?" Cynthia replied, "Yes, I would, because I'm not the one to judge what his path is. We don't know each other's paths; we have to let fate take its course. I'm not budging on thirty. I am not willing to surrender my honest beliefs. If the judge sentences him to death, then that's not my call. I will not take responsibility for that." The last thing I remember was Steve's tired voice saying, "Well, it seems to me then, there's no real purpose of going around the room anymore."

After three days of intense personal and group struggle, we agreed to declare ourselves a hung jury. Many of us felt a deep sense of failure about not performing the duty we'd been assigned. But when it comes to a matter of life and death, it's not easy for twelve people to agree. The judge eventually decided on a sentence of two consecutive life terms without parole for Matthew Dawson.

EPILOGUE

I never met my fellow jurors again. But three months after the trial, I came across the following posting on a blog that covered the trial proceedings. It was supposedly a post from Cynthia Jansen.

> I read your article about the Dawson case. It still bothers me even today. I'm Juror #12. It would appear that the world lets people die because of the mistakes they make. That, to me, is incredibly sad. I think I would be killed if the other eleven jurors were to judge me by my mistakes in life. I knew deep down I was so wrong signing the guilty verdict. I just gave up. If someone would not have crumbled as I did, I wish they would have taken my place on that jury. —Cynthia

KEY TERMS

communication competence   leadership

decision making   problem solving

interdependence   roles

DISCUSSION QUESTIONS

1. What are the bases for the various jurors' arguments? Are these appropriate?

2. How well do these jury members balance personal decision-making with group decision-making during deliberation? That is, how do they try to achieve the balance between arriving at the best decision, arriving at a unanimous decision, and arriving at a decision that agrees with personal conscience?

3. What is the role of rational argument versus value-based (or personal) argument in a jury decision-making situation?

4. Why do some group discussions reach an impasse? What strategies would have helped this jury dislodge from its impasse? Could those strategies be used in other groups as well?

5. Is unanimity a good decision rule for juries? Or would it be better to allow a majority or a 2/3rds vote? What do you think is the best decision rule for juries, and why?

6. How would you evaluate the leadership in this case? Was the foreman effective? Why or why not? If you were the elected foreperson in this jury, what might you have done differently (if anything)?

CONTEMPLATING PATIENT COMPETENCY

Exploring Ethical Group Decision Making on a Hospital Ethics Committee Board

Heather J. Carmack

A health care team discusses whether a patient should be capable of refusing further cancer treatment.

At 7:45 in the morning, Urban Hospital was already bustling, patients signing in for their 8:00 appointments and taking seats in the waiting area. Jeannie Anderson poured herself a cup of coffee from her small office coffee maker and sat at her desk to go over the day's agenda. As the head of Urban Hospital's legal department, Jeannie's days were usually packed with meetings, depositions, and case reviews. Today, she also had an Ethics Committee Board (ECB) meeting to discuss a patient's cancer treatment. She turned her attention to the case for that morning's meeting involving Captain David Brown. As she read over the case file, she sighed. Another challenging case was on the agenda, and it did not look as if it would have a quick and easy answer.

DEFINING THE CASE

Captain Brown was a 75-year-old male who had served in both the Korean and Vietnam wars. Like many Vietnam veterans, Captain Brown suffered from posttraumatic stress disorder, which only recently had been declared a disorder by the military. Captain Brown had suffered from nightmares and occasional mild delusions, often manifesting in paranoid beliefs that people were "out to get him." Captain Brown was particularly suspicious of anyone involved in the military, especially military doctors, because of their constant denial of his posttraumatic stress. After several years of therapy, Captain Brown's nightmares and delusions stopped.

Three years ago, Captain Brown visited his family general practitioner, complaining of short-ness of breath and chest pain. His doctor ordered tests and chest X-rays and discovered a mass on Captain Brown's lung. The oncology team, headed by Dr. Adams, discovered that Captain Brown had stage III lung cancer. Dr. Adams suggested that Captain Brown immediately begin an aggressive treatment that included both chemotherapy and radiation. Initially, the treatment worked, the lung tumor began to shrink in size, and Captain Brown went into remission. A year and a half after the original diagnosis, the cancer returned, this time spreading to his stomach. Again, Dr. Adams suggested chemotherapy and radiation. At this time, Captain Brown, under the advice of Dr. Adams, signed a health care proxy. The health care proxy passes the authority to make one's own health care decisions to another adult when one has become incapacitated or is unable to make one's own decisions. Captain Brown named his daughter his health care agent in the event that he became too sick from the cancer or cancer treatments to make decisions. He also signed an advance directive stating that he did not want extraordinary measures, such as life support.

Five months ago, Captain Brown began forgetting his treatment and doctor appointments. He also became disoriented and would talk to family members and his doctors as if they were members of his old platoon. Dr. Adams, knowing about Captain Brown's previous experience with posttraumatic stress, sent Captain Brown to the hospital's mental disorders department. During his meeting with a psychiatric resident, Captain Brown was lucid and was able to answer questions clearly. The resident, however, was still concerned because family members and other doctors reported disorientation and delusional episodes. After their meeting, the resident called for a neurology consult. The neurologist looked over Captain Brown's MRI scan and declared that Captain Brown had what looked like the beginning stages of Alzheimer's disease. The psychiatry resident came to the same conclusion: Captain Brown had Alzheimer's. Together, the psychiatry resident and neurologist told Captain Brown and his daughter that he had Alzheimer's and suggested that he begin taking a popular Alzheimer's medication. Two weeks later, Captain Brown told Dr. Adams that he wanted to stop his cancer treatment.

After reading Captain Brown's file, Jeannie thought about the different ethical dilemmas presented in this case. First, Captain Brown's case was complicated by the fact that he had signed a health proxy document. Complicating matters even further was the fact that Captain Brown's daughter did not support her father's decision to end his cancer treatment. Finally, Captain Brown's diagnosis of Alzheimer's further impacted the decision. Captain Brown's psychiatrist and neurologist questioned whether he was competent enough to make this decision. Not knowing what to do, Dr. Adams contacted Jeannie to set up an ethics committee board meeting in order to determine Captain Brown's competency.

ETHICAL DECISION MAKING AND THE ETHICS COMMITTEE BOARD

Two floors down, Dr. Moore, Urban Hospital's chief of staff, opened up Captain Brown's case file. As he read over the case, Dr. Moore thought about the complexities of the case and how this case was so different from the first ECB case. Originally, the ECB was a policy that encouraged physicians to engage in peer discussion of difficult cases and decisions. At first, physicians were hesitant to talk to one another about difficult cases for fear of being seen as lacking knowledge and of being called into court if a difficult case went to trial. That quickly changed after the first ECB case was a success.

Dr. Moore had heard stories about the first ECB case. Doctors were conflicted about whether to take a young patient off life support after he suffered brain damage during a car accident, because there was evidence that the patient's brain was healing. The then-chief of staff gathered together all the treating physicians and nurses as well as several administrators to work through the medical and ethical issues and find a solution. The chief of staff was impressed by the group's ability to work together to find a solution and how each person brought a different perspective to the discussion. The chief of staff thought the group interaction was so successful that he officially established the ECB, calling on hospital staff and administrators to meet when presented with a complicated case. Dr. Moore shook his head; like Captain Brown's case, the first ECB case asked physicians, nurses, and administrators to wrestle with several complex ethical issues in order to make a decision.

The ECB board consisted of several permanent members: Jeannie, Dr. Moore, Becky, the paralegal, the chiefs of every hospital department, the head of nursing, and a patient advocate. All other nurses, physicians, and administrators were "floating" members, meaning that they were only involved if the case involved their service or if they could offer expert insight about the case. Patients and patients' families were invited to participate in the committee meetings, as well. Dr. Moore thought about how his role had changed with the ECB; when he first started at Urban Hospital, he was a floating member, becoming a permanent member when he became chief of staff. One of the things Dr. Moore liked about the ECB was how everyone's opinions and knowledge were considered in the decision-making process, and he made sure to give everyone who attended an ECB meeting an opportunity to share his or her perspectives.

Dr. Moore read over the notes on the case, thinking about what would happen in the meeting. The ECB only met when the urgency of a case required it. Once convened, the committee discussed the facts of the case, identifying concrete information and highlighting the ethical dilemmas. The committee dealt with decision making and problem solving, as some cases focus on selecting a solution while others need solutions created. For example, the ECB recently had to make a decision about how the hospital was going to handle changes in the hospital's living will document and how those changes would affect active living wills. Becky took copious notes during the meeting, which were later transcribed and placed in the patients' files. Copies of the notes were sent to the patients, ensuring that everyone involved had a copy. Decisions made in an ECB meeting were not final decisions, but rather were meant to be a chance for dialogue and discussion. Physicians were encouraged to wait forty-eight hours to make a final decision in order to reflect on the meeting and the implications of their decision.

WORKING TOWARD A DECISION

Jeannie finished reading over the medical records and case file for the ethics committee meeting. Gathering her papers and filling her coffee cup once more, she headed to the elevator. Jeannie entered the conference room to find seven physicians already present, huddled around the coffee, doughnuts, and pastries. The conference room was set up with a projector and screen so that physicians could show files and X-rays during their discussion. As Jeannie took a seat, the other physicians, nurses, and the patient advocate on the ECB walked into the room. Today's meeting was going to be packed.

The conference room door opened again; Captain Brown and his daughter, Ann, walked in. Dr. Adams walked over to Captain Brown, and shook his hand. "Good morning, Captain. How are you this morning?" he asked as he guided him to a chair.

"I'm doing just fine, Doctor. I'm having a pretty good day so far. Hope it stays that way," the captain responded, sitting down.

Dr. Adams started the meeting. "Captain Brown, Ann, this is Dr. Moore, the chief of staff, and Jeannie Anderson, head of the legal department. This is Becky, the paralegal. She is going to be taking notes today. You already know just about everyone else, so why don't we get started? We are here to decide if Captain Brown is competent enough to make the decision to end his cancer treatment. Captain Brown, what we are going to do is have each physician present his or her knowledge of the case so that we all have a full picture of what we are dealing with. As the oncologist, I can only speak about the course of treatment for cancer, but that is a big part of the decision here. Captain Brown is receiving treatment for the reappearance of lung cancer. The cancer is advanced; however, the treatments have made an impact."

Dr. Adams motioned to one of the oncology team members and an image of Captain Brown's lungs appeared on the projector screen. "As you can see here," said Dr. Adams, "there are three average-sized tumors in his right lung. The tumors have made it difficult for Captain Brown to breathe. When we discovered that the cancer had returned, I advised Captain Brown to sign a health care proxy document and an advance directive in case he could no longer make medical decisions because of the cancer or consequences of the treatments." Dr. Adams continued to explain Captain Brown's case, talking about his type of cancer and his current treatment regimen.

The neurologist jumped in after Dr. Adams, explaining the neurological aspects of the case. "I met Captain Brown about five months ago after I was called to consult on an MRI. At that time, I observed that Captain Brown was lucid and could clearly talk about his health. However, I know that his daughter and Dr. Adams reported that he sometimes is disoriented and forgets things." The MRI appeared on the projector screen. "I observed in the MRI early signs of Alzheimer's. However, he is responding well to the Alzheimer's medication."

The psychiatrist echoed the neurologist, stating that in her meetings with Captain Brown, he was normally very lucid. Dr. Moore and Jeannie knew that this was the overarching tension in the case. Even though his daughter and Dr. Adams reported bouts of confusion and forgetfulness, the neurologist and psychiatrist did not observe those moments. It was going to come down to whether all the committee members decided Captain Brown was lucid enough to make a decision.

After all physicians presented their parts of the case, Dr. Adams turned to Captain Brown and Ann. "Do either of you want to add anything?"

Captain Brown paused for a moment and then spoke. "I want to end my cancer treatment. The first round of treatment was awful. I lost a lot of weight, I couldn't eat, I was tired all the time. I don't want to do it again. I think this cancer coming back means that maybe it's my time."

Ann cut him off. "Dad, don't say that. Just because the cancer is back doesn't mean that you should die."

"Annie, don't start this again. I know the best decision here. I want to end my treatment and I should be able to!" shouted Captain Brown.

Jeannie decided that since the decision was in part compounded by the health care proxy document that Captain Brown signed, she would add her legal expertise to the discussion. "I think part of the problem is the signing of the health care proxy. If Captain Brown hadn't signed this, we wouldn't be having a hard time here. I looked over the document and it's a standard document that states that health care decisions go to Ann if Captain Brown becomes unable to make decisions. Legally, we just need to determine if Captain Brown is lucid enough now to make this decision."

Ann spoke up. "But Dr. Adams says that the treatments are making an impact. You could still beat the cancer like last time, Dad. Why don't you want to try?"

The psychiatrist answered Ann. "Ann, I think part of the reason that you are reluctant to end your father's treatment is that maybe you are afraid to let your father go."

Dr. Moore watched as Ann and Captain Brown quietly looked at each other. Finally, he thought, the real reason that Ann is fighting this decision: She is not ready for her dad to die. However, emotions did not always matter once legal documents were signed. Regardless of how Ann and Captain Brown felt, it was up to the doctors to determine if he was competent enough to end his treatment. Dr. Moore broke the silence. "Captain Brown, do you understand what will happen if you choose to end treatment?"

"Not really. I told Dr. Adams that I didn't want to hear any of that in case he was trying to persuade me otherwise." He paused. "What would happen?"

"Well," said Dr. Adams, "we would stop the chemo and radiation immediately. It would take a little while to get the chemo out of your system, and you would still probably have the same side effects: vomiting, weight loss, that sort of thing." He paused. "The cancer would start to eat away your lungs and stomach. The cancer might spread to other parts of your body, most likely your pancreas. We could give you morphine for the pain, but it would still be painful. Eventually, you would have trouble breathing. We could give you oxygen, but since you signed an advance directive, we wouldn't intubate you if you stopped breathing. Eventually, it would be difficult for you to breathe and you would just stop."

Ann turned to her father, tears in her eyes. "Dad, is that what you want? To not be able to breathe?"

Captain Brown took a deep breath and looked at Dr. Adams. "How long would I have left?"

"Maybe three months, maybe more. I don't really know how fast the cancer will advance or how your body will respond once we stop the treatment."

The other doctors sat quietly as Dr. Adams spoke. When he finished, the patient advocate asked if Ann and Captain Brown understood everything that Dr. Adams and the other doctors had said. On the surface, this meeting was to decide if the physicians thought Captain Brown was competent to end his cancer treatment. This meeting also served, however, as a way for Captain Brown to decide if he truly *wanted* to end his cancer treatment.

Dr. Adams turned to the neurologist. "What do you think? How much longer until Captain Brown's Alzheimer's is too advanced to make decisions? Do you think that Captain Brown is competent enough to make this decision?"

"It's hard to tell how Alzheimer's will advance and how fast. As I said, he is responding well to the medication. Based on what I've seen, I think that Captain Brown is lucid enough to make this decision." The psychiatrist echoed the neurologist's statement.

"I do have one concern," said Captain Brown. "Would I have to end the Alzheimer's treatment if I ended the cancer treatment? I don't want to be dying from cancer and be crazy."

"I don't see why you couldn't continue the treatment," said the neurologist. "However, I don't know if the cancer will have an impact on the Alzheimer's, especially if the cancer moves to your brain."

Captain Brown sat in silence, shaking his head slowly in understanding. "What about you, Dr. Adams? What do you think?"

Dr. Adams paused. "Well, I think that if the neurologist thinks that the Alzheimer's hasn't advanced too far, then you should be able to make the decision. But I still have a hard time saying it's okay to end your treatment when you are making progress. We still have a shot to beat this thing."

Dr. Moore signaled Dr. Adams to conclude the meeting. "I think we still have a lot to think about. Captain Brown, we need some time to think about this and we will let you know what we decide."

KEY TERMS

decision making   problem solving

ethics   relational communication

group boundaries   roles

power

DISCUSSION QUESTIONS

1. What ethical issues does the ECB need to consider when making their decision about Captain Brown's case?

2. What role does relational communication have in this case? To what extent should relational concerns be influential when making ethical decisions?

3. What informal roles are present in the ECB case? Why it is important to have informal roles in the ECB?

4. What kind of power do you see evident in this case? Identify three different types of power exhibited by different members of the group.

5. How do the ECB members determine the criteria for evaluating Captain Brown's case?

6. What are the advantages and disadvantages of the ECB's decision-making process?

7. How does the EBC work to achieve consensus? What can other groups learn from the events in this case?

case 18

UTILIZING TEAM MEMBER EXPERTISE UNDER PRESSURE

Heidi K. Gardner and Erin McFee

A business consulting team struggles to function under increased scrutiny.

"What's with all these data requests?" asked Julia Narino, leafing through the stack of papers Sid Vannick had just handed her. "Let's hold off on these until we get the word from the client."

Julia was second-in-command of a Wilson Associates consulting team. Their task was to help Pinewood, a London-based extreme sports retail chain, expand its American business from the East Coast and Midwest into the Rockies. The team leader, Tomas Raima, was out of town, but that shouldn't have mattered. Julia was Wilson Associates' acknowledged expert on Pinewood and it was her responsibility to oversee the data collection and analysis carried out by the four analysts who were junior members of the team. Julia had worked with this important client on three other successful projects over the last four years and had earned the trust of its CEO, Paolo Calla, and other top executives.

"Tomas wants this research done for his presentation in New York," answered Sid, one of her analysts.

"No, no, it's a waste of time," answered Julia. "I know these guys. They're not going to move forward until they know London is on board. All we need now is an executive summary for Paolo. If he wants changes, we'll have wasted time and money jumping the gun with this research. And believe me, the clients won't like that."

Julia paused for a moment, wondering why Tomas would have asked for such studies in the first place; that was her job. Then she noticed that Sid wasn't answering. In fact, all four of her analysts were looking back and forth at each other. "Okay," said Sid. "We'll see if that's okay with Tomas."

Julia got up from her chair and was about to answer, but stopped herself just in time. What was going on here? Everybody knew she was the expert on how to move things through the Pinewood hierarchy. Tomas himself was the first to acknowledge it, and he had publicly done just that at the outset of the project. Why weren't they listening to her now?

A SPECIAL CLIENT

Julia Narino had been at Wilson Associates, a retail-strategy consulting firm, for four years with; next year she would be a candidate for partnership. At Wilson Associates, as at most professional service firms, the competition for partnership was intense—every few years you either got promoted or took the hint and looked for another firm. The system could be brutal but the results were impressive. Those who made partner were very good at providing their clients with tangible success. When a partner led a team working on a client project, the nonpartner members of that team were inspired to give their best, partly to improve their own chances for partnership but also out of genuine respect for their team leader.

Pinewood was the leading extreme sports retailer in Europe and was trying to become a leader in the United States. It was a pioneer in "experience centers," or what the Europeans called "retailtainment." At a Pinewood outlet, you could not only buy extreme sports equipment but also try it out in a skating park or a wave machine or on a rock-climbing wall. Working with Wilson Associates, and particularly with Julia, Pinewood had already established itself in the Northeast and Midwest of the United States. Julia had built up a good rapport with Pinewood executives. They trusted her and, thanks to her familiarity with the company's complex operational, financial, and political structures, she was able to get things done.

Although every consultant wants to cultivate a good relationship with his or her clients, Julia was particularly motivated to do so at Pinewood. Here was a successful retailer that was ambitious to grow and eager to innovate—a retail-strategy consultant's dream. Also, strong relationships with A-list clients like Pinewood were one of the critical requirements of partnership.

A GOOD PROJECT

Every person on the team had a crucial role in devising Pinewood's expansion strategy. Tomas Raima was an expert on real estate acquisition and management for growing retail chains. He had only recently become a partner; this was his first project in that new role. Julia was the senior project manager, which meant that, while Tomas was responsible for keeping in touch with the client's needs and expectations, she was responsible for keeping the project moving internally, making sure each of her analysts did his or her part and that they all worked together. She might drop in on analyst Carla Burns, for example, and say, "Before you start calling Pinewood's suppliers, check in with Sid because he has to call some of them, too. No use bugging them with separate calls and making it look like we're disorganized." Every phase of a project like this required frequent communication, regular meetings, and team-level analysis.

Julia had been quite pleased with this assignment. She was always happy to work with Pinewood, and she was also happy for a chance to work with Tomas. He was something of a rising star at Wilson Associates. Clients were already requesting him by name and he was generally considered to be a good person to work with. A successful project with him could give her the boost she needed to make partner herself next year.

At the first team meeting, Tomas told the group: "We're lucky to have Julia on this team. She knows more about who's who and what's what at Pinewood than anyone in our firm, probably more than some folks at Pinewood know about themselves. They trust her because she's done great work for them. So let's make the most of that. If Julia says this is how to get something done there, you don't need to check it with me."

Both leaders were adept at helping the rest of the team members work together. They jointly decided to begin meetings with what Tomas called a "spaghetti session," in which each team member had a chance to "throw the spaghetti against the wall and see what sticks." Ideas were rigorously critiqued, but team members were quick to notice that their ideas were taken seriously and sometimes became part of the Pinewood expansion strategy.

THE TEAM TAKES A HIT

Ten weeks into the fourteen-week schedule, the project was going well. Then, Great Outdoors, the leading outdoor sporting goods retailer in the United States and one of Pinewood's direct U.S. competitors, dropped a bomb. It planned to open a chain of "X-Centers" throughout the Rockies region. These retail stores would have skateboard parks, rock-climbing walls, and virtual-reality mountaineering simulations.

The next day, Tomas found a message on his voicemail from Rick Dale, one of Wilson Associate's senior partners. "Heard about the Great Outdoors debacle from Paolo. I'm sure you know how critical our Pinewood connection is to everyone's bottom line. And I mean everyone's. This isn't one any of us can afford to lose, Tomas, so straighten her out and land the plane."

Soon, Tomas was on the phone to Julia. "How on earth did this slip by?" he demanded.

Of course, the team had carried out a competitive analysis in order to determine what competition Pinewood might face—now or in the future—in its Rockies expansion, and Great Outdoors had been a focal point in that analysis. As senior project manager, Julia had overseen that analysis and, in her view, it had been a thorough job. Tomas seemed to have been impressed, too.

Julia tried not to sound defensive. "I don't know what happened. I know we did our homework. We talked to everybody and nobody knew this was coming." She thought for a moment. "Look, Tomas, Great Outdoors decided to keep this top, top secret and—hats off to them—they pulled it off. We'll retrace our steps, but offhand I just can't think of anything we did wrong."

"We may not have done anything wrong, but we sure as hell blew it," Tomas replied.

Julia was torn between consoling Tomas—his first assignment as a partner was already blowing up in his face—and defending the project team.

"No one at Pinewood had any idea, either, and it's their own necks. So Paolo can't be too hard on us for missing it. Remember, Pinewood is big and growing. The Rockies expansion may hit some turbulence, but it's not going to crash. Pinewood will win in the end because this is their game. Great Outdoors can play at being extreme, but what they know is tennis racquets and golf balls. Once customers have a chance to compare stores in the same area—and you know that's just what these extreme types love to blog about—Pinewood will be fine. We're going to stick to our guns and give them the best possible strategy to expand *successfully and permanently*, not necessarily immediately or effortlessly."

It took a moment for Tomas to reply. "I don't know, Julia. I've got Dale and the other partners breathing down my neck. And Paolo isn't quite as fair-minded as you think. Who did he call when it hit the fan? The senior partners. Not me. Not even you."

THE TEAM LOSES ITS NERVE

A week later, the whole team was gathered for its Wednesday update. As had been the case for the last few meetings, Tomas had skipped the "spaghetti session."

"All right," he began, "give me what you have." Julia noticed how anxious the team members were, not only to show off their work, but also to one-up each other. Carla Burns, the analyst after presenting her projections for tourism in the Rockies over the next five years, added: "This is what's going to matter most for Pinewood." In fact, Julia noted, Carla had missed an important issue. Although it was certainly Julia's role to point such things out, she and Tomas had always preferred to let the analysts critique each other as much as possible. It was good training, it developed their self-confidence, and, as long as the team leaders kept things under control, the mutual criticism helped build camaraderie and improved the team's work. Julia glanced over at Tomas, but he was staring down at his BlackBerry. She looked over to Nick Bluefield. He was a sharp analyst and had always been a gold mine of helpful critique; she was sure he had noticed what was missing from Carla's presentation. Nick glanced over at Tomas, but Tomas scooped up his stack of reports and stood up. "I have to go," he announced. "I'll look these over and let you know."

Let us know what? Julia wondered.

As the lunch break began, Julia pulled Nick aside. "I know, I know," he said, before she could even begin. "Listen, I want to make partner as much as you do, but I'm nowhere near as close to it as you are. I don't know what's got into Tomas, but it's his project. I can't afford to make waves."

"But that's your job," Julia replied. "I know Pinewood inside and out, and Tomas knows retail and real estate inside and out, but there's always a need for someone like you who can keep the rest of us on our toes. There was some sloppy work in this meeting, but I didn't hear the kind of critique I'm used to hearing in this group. Come on, Nick, we owe it to Pinewood not to give them something half-baked, even if they accept it." She stopped herself from saying, "Even if Tomas accepts it."

"Maybe," answered Nick, "but the other partners have made it clear this is an important project. I'm lucky to be on it, but there's a reason why you guys are in charge and I'm only an analyst. Tomas may be acting a little weird, but I have to figure he knows what he's doing. I think we'll do fine and I'm not going to be the one who's always in the way."

Before the meeting resumed, Julia took Carla aside. "Before you finish off your report, Carla, you need to look into the spillover from the other business units. Bring it up to the group and I'm sure you'll get some good feedback. It's the kind of thing the other analysts need to think about, too." But Carla didn't bring it up and Julia let it pass, having decided to look into the other units herself.

OUT IN THE COLD

Julia handed the stack of data requests back to Sid Vannick and sat back down. So, they weren't going to take her advice on an executive summary for Paolo until Tomas said it was okay? Julia wasn't even angry as much as she was baffled. Shouldn't they know they were taking the wrong step, considering that Julia knew what she was talking about? Why did they need to check with Tomas when he had told them from the start that she would be spearheading exactly this kind of research? She knew better than anyone who made which decisions at Pinewood and who needed to know what.

When she got back to her office, there was an e-mail from Tomas. The subject line said "yesterday's update with Pinewood"—a meeting Julia hadn't even known was going to happen. Tomas had attached the slides he had presented to Pinewood's executive team in the company's New York headquarters. To her shock, it was all standard stuff, right out of the Wilson Associates playbook, with nothing to indicate that it had been tailored for Pinewood. Where were all the good ideas she and the rest of the team had come up with to match Pinewood's unique corporate culture and market position? Even some of Tomas's most interesting ideas had been washed away. Julia knew full well that Paolo would be deeply disappointed. This wasn't at all what he had come to expect from Wilson Associates.

Julia was appalled, embarrassed, and angry. She had not spent four years cultivating a unique and productive relationship with a really interesting and ambitious company just to have her name associated with a third-rate presentation like this. She wasn't afraid to talk things out with Tomas, but she was afraid that it might do more harm than good. He wasn't as open with her—or with anyone on the team—as he used to be. With only two weeks left to complete the project, there wouldn't be much time to restore their working relationship if the discussion went badly. A breakdown in team relations now would do a great disservice to Pinewood, to Wilson Associates, to Tomas, to her analysts, and to herself.

She could imagine saying to Tomas, "Look, just because we made one bad mistake in the competitive analysis doesn't mean we have to make a bunch more. We *know* how to do this right. Let's do it." On the other hand, maybe she should just go with the flow and do everything in her power to keep the ideas rolling, keep the team working together, and present Pinewood with a great strategy—then try to figure out afterwards what had gone wrong.

But she was worried that, the way things were going, Pinewood would be offered an inferior expansion strategy—one with her name on it.

KEY TERMS

Conflict	leadership
Expertise use	meetings
interdependence	power
influences on group tasks and activities	working under pressure

DISCUSSION QUESTIONS

1. What influences on group tasks and activities are evident in this case? What happened to the team dynamics as pressures on the team increased?

2. What are possible reasons for why the analysts and project manager were less responsive to Julia's suggestions in recent meetings?

3. What role did status play in the changing group dynamics? What power bases are different group members drawing on in this case?

4. Assess the behavior of the team members. What was their goal when they started the project? Did that change? If so, how? How did their actions support their goals?

5. What conflict management styles do you see evident in this case? How could things have changed if members had exhibited a different approach to conflict?

6. Analyze Julia's options: what should she do? What are the risks and trade-offs for your recommendation for Julia?

FIXING SCHOOLS BY TELLING LIES?

The Case of the Helping Hands Organization

Sarah Stawiski

Students in a community service group face an ethical dilemma in their efforts to help inprove local schools.

"I knew it seemed too good to be true," exclaimed Travis as he walked into the student union at State College on Thursday morning with Miles. Travis, Miles, and two other students on the fundraising subcommittee of their organization, Helping Hands, were facing an unexpected kink in their plans, and an emergency meeting had been called to decide how to handle it.

Helping Hands was a student organization on campus whose mission was to fix up schools to create a better learning environment for children in the community. Groups of college students went to schools on the weekends to paint, clean, repair broken windows and desks, build basketball courts, clear outdoor play areas, and do other odd jobs to help schools with limited resources. They provided assistance to elementary schools, middle schools, and high schools. Since State College was located in a large urban environment, there were plenty of schools with funding shortages in need of help.

The fundraising subcommittee had been planning their big annual event to raise money for their organization. The money raised would be used to support the organization's social agenda, such as recruiting parties, as well as transportation for the group to get to the schools and other supplies and materials that they might need. The plan was to sell tickets to a music event that would be held on campus.

The event had been scheduled for some time, but since the Helping Hands events subcommittee hadn't been able to sell many tickets at the original price, they had to offer the tickets at a major discount. They were on the verge of making no money at all for Helping Hands and were actually worried they might take a loss. About ten days before the event, an alumnus of the organization was able to call in a favor to have a well-known pop star, Gianna, agree to appear at the event. Gianna would sing a few songs at the event since she had grown up in the area and appreciated what the students were doing for the local schools. The organizers were ecstatic and decided to raise additional funds by raffling off tickets for the chance to meet Gianna in person before the show.

On Sunday night, less than a week before the big event and just one day before starting to sell raffle tickets, the students were contacted by Gianna's agent, who told them there was a 70 percent chance that Gianna would have to cancel due to illness. The agent said there was still hope that she would recover, and they wouldn't cancel definitively until the day of the show. The students knew that without Gianna, there would be no way to raffle off tickets to earn extra money for the event.

On Monday morning, an emergency meeting was called just an hour before they were scheduled to start selling tickets. The group decided to meet at the beginning of the day to decide how to handle the situation—most importantly, whether they should still sell raffle tickets, and whether they should be honest about the chance that Gianna—the star attraction—might not make it.

Travis and Miles walked to an empty table to discuss the matter privately. Just as they sat down, Annie and Sofia walked in and joined them.

"Well, aren't we lucky? We get to deal with this little issue just a week before finals start!" complained Annie with a sarcastic smile.

Everyone took off their backpacks and settled in at the table.

Travis started the meeting. "Well, just to make sure everyone at this table has heard the news—I got a call last night from Gianna's agent notifying us that Gianna is sick with the flu and she has had to cancel her last two shows. He wanted to let us know that there is a good chance Gianna won't be able to make it this weekend." Travis wanted to make sure everyone was on the same page. "And in less than an hour, we're going to have people lining up to buy raffle tickets from us and we need to make some quick decisions."

The group members looked at one other for a second before Sofia spoke up. "Well, this just isn't fair. Should we call her back and see how she's feeling today? Maybe she's doing better." Sofia was particularly disappointed about this news because she had worked really hard on the fundraiser this year and she wanted it to be a success. She was already daydreaming about her first job interview when she would impress her potential employer by telling them how much money she had raised for the organization.

Travis was already shaking his head. "It was clear from the agent that he'd contact us on Friday by the end of the day and no decisions would be made before then."

"I guess we should just postpone ticket sales until we know for sure," suggested Annie.

"I guess that might be the only option at this point," said Miles reluctantly, trying to make eye contact with the rest of the group to see if anyone disagreed.

Travis frowned and tapped his finger on the table, clearly frustrated. "If we do that, we won't raise any money this year. Almost all of our service events will have to be scratched next year! We've already made promises to those schools. Plus, without being able to host any social events, it's hard to recruit new members to Helping Hands. We need all the help we can get."

The fall recruitment party was a big deal for Helping Hands. A lot of the other campus organizations had more money because they had been around longer and were therefore able to rent out impressive venues in the city and to hire popular entertainment. At the beginning of each school year, organizations competed for the interest of incoming students who wanted to attend the best events. Helping Hands wouldn't be able to get new students to come and learn about their organization by throwing a couple of bags of chips on a table and turning on the iPod. Plus, it was a time for the current members to kick back and have some fun in order to gear up for the hard work they would do throughout the school year.

"Not to mention the fact that Education Angels just had their most successful fundraiser ever! We're going to look like total losers. We've been better than them every year. I'm not about to let them win now," Miles pointed out.

The rivalry with Education Angels, another organization on campus, which collected toys and supplies and donated them to schools in need, was always a point of discussion. Some of the members of Helping Hands resented that Education Angels seemed to get more publicity, although their members never "got their hands dirty." A former member of Education Angels had gone to work for a local newspaper after graduation and was able to get them a lot of local media coverage. Many of the students of Helping Hands felt that Education Angels just collected things and delivered them to the schools, had their photo op, and left.

"I mean, I really wanted to raise a lot of money this year, but I guess it's just not our year. Maybe we can do some other fundraising over the summer," suggested Annie, trying to stay positive about the situation.

The members of the group grew silent at the realization that most members would be returning to their home towns this summer, leaving no time for additional fundraising.

"Okay, I have a great idea," Miles said, laughing. Miles had the reputation of having a way of putting others at ease, even in uncomfortable situations like these. "Let's not say a word about Gianna not coming. Then, when we announce the winners, we just tell them that they have to meet her blindfolded. We'll chalk it up to her being a diva. We'll play a video of her talking and we'll get Sofia to shake their hands. They'll never know the difference!"

The whole group laughed with Miles.

Travis kept the joke going. "Yeah, I mean, we never said how we are defining 'meet!' What if we just have her call in on the phone? Meet-by-teleconference!"

"Or a life-size photo of her where you can get your picture taken," added Sofia, still laughing. The group laughed again and then was silent. Each member looked down momentarily and then slyly looked around the table to see how others were reacting.

With a sly half-smile on her face, Sofia questioned the group cautiously. "Well, I mean, do we *have* to tell them she might not be coming? I mean, when we sell a raffle ticket, it's for the *chance* to meet Gianna, it's not a sure thing anyway! It's not like we're selling $100 tickets, we're selling $1 raffle tickets. It's kind of like we're just taking whatever chance they had that their raffle ticket would be selected and cutting that chance a little more— not only do you have to get selected, you have to hope that Gianna shows up!"

The group laughed again.

Travis, more seriously now, chimed in. "Well, in a way, that's true. It's not like the whole event is cancelled, it's just one of the performers and the chance of meeting her before the show. And we don't know *for sure* that she *isn't* coming. There is still a really good chance that she'll be there. I mean, how long does the flu last, anyway? If she's already taken two days off, I'm sure she's well rested by now!"

Sofia and Miles seemed to be thinking it through and nodded their heads in agreement. Annie frowned and squinted her eyes at the group, trying to make sense of what they were saying. "I don't know, guys, I'd probably want to know ahead of time what my actual chances of meeting Gianna are before I bought a ticket. It seems like we should probably be up front about this. Couldn't we just tell people when they come to buy tickets that Gianna might not be able to make it after all, but they are still helping a good cause either way?"

"Well, that's just it!" Miles interrupted. "We are selling a *chance* to meet her, but even before this happened, we couldn't tell people what their chances were because we didn't know for sure how many people would end up purchasing tickets. So, in essence, nothing has changed."

Annie was still skeptical. "But what would happen if people find out we're lying? Won't we get in trouble?"

Travis, the president of Helping Hands and chair of the fundraising subcommittee, had a lot of influence in this group. He was well respected for his devotion to the work. While most members of the organization rotated to get in two to three work events per semester, Travis attended almost all of them, usually about ten a semester. Feeling responsible for the group, Travis began to worry a little bit about getting the whole organization in trouble over this. "Well, remember what happened to Alpha Chi last year? They told everyone they were using money from a fundraiser to help a homeless shelter, then we found out they used the money to rent limos for the winter formal! They were put on probation for a year and no one wants to be associated with them anymore."

Miles was the first to respond. "Well, what *they* did is a little different, though. We're not exactly going to be spending any money on limos and winter formals."

Travis's story made Annie even more nervous. "I heard some of the girls lost their scholarships after that, too. And remember the Dean making that announcement that dishonesty in fundraising wouldn't be tolerated? There are pretty strict rules around fundraising, guys. Just keep that in mind."

Sofia answered in almost a whisper. "Those girls are just plain stupid. They are nothing like *us*. Any anyway, nobody except the four of us knows about the call from the agent, right? So, if she ends up cancelling, we can just pretend it was just one of those last-minute cancellations that was out of our hands. I mean, we can't get in trouble for *her* getting sick."

Everyone but Annie nodded their heads in agreement and sat up in their seats.

Travis's face of defeat changed to one of excitement. "Besides, what's the big harm in a few students 'wasting' a dollar or two on a raffle ticket, if you even want to call it 'wasting,' when their money will be going to helping to fix up some of the poorest schools in the area? Think of the kids in those schools. They are counting on us. I personally have no issues with delaying the news if it means that we can help more kids next year."

Miles agreed. "That's a good point—if we get caught, we'll tell everyone we're just like Robin Hood. Everyone loves Robin Hood!"

The group laughed again.

Sofia added, "I know! Those people typically spend a lot more on their beer fund every week than they are going to spend on these raffle tickets. If partying is so important to them and they can't be bothered to come out and help kids that really need it, I personally have no problem with taking a few of their dollars so that at least someone can go and do something meaningful other than getting wasted at some party."

Sofia's attitude toward the students who were not members of Helping Hands was pretty typical. A lot of the members felt that their own values were different from the values of students who chose not to join Helping Hands. Some especially bitter members had a saying, "Helping Hands helped some kids today while the rest of you slept your life away." The common stereotype was that nonmembers prefer to spend the weekends partying late and sleeping in instead of getting up early to help fix up schools all day.

"*And*, there are still two bands that are definitely coming. I'm sure Jerry's cousins, who are in one of the other bands, would be willing to do a meet-and-greet before the show, so it's not like the raffle winners would get *nothing*. It's just not necessarily going to be meeting Gianna," added Travis, becoming more sure that they shouldn't say anything about the possible cancellation.

"I don't know, I mean, it seems a little . . . unethical?" Annie was clearly uncomfortable with where this meeting was going. As the newest member of the group, however, she was worried that she would offend her new friends.

"Well, it might actually be more unethical to say anything at all since we just don't have all the facts yet. If Gianna calls it off for sure, then we should tell people. For now, there is no harm in just saying nothing. It's not like we're lying, we're just not going to disclose that information since it is still up in the air," replied Travis gently.

"But if Gianna calls it off completely Friday or Saturday, all the tickets will be sold. We're announcing the raffle winners on Friday afternoon. It will be too late," says Annie.

"Annie, no offense, but it seems like you don't really get what we're saying. I know you are trying to do what you think is right, but protecting the work of Helping Hands is also the right thing to do. And like Travis said, we aren't going to lie, we're just going to delay disclosing the information until we know for sure," said Sofia somewhat impatiently.

"Well, if that's what you all want to do, I'm not going to stop you, I just don't know . . ." responded Annie.

Travis liked Annie and didn't want the newest member of the group to feel uncomfortable. "Annie, I have an idea, why don't you just take the week off from selling tickets. We don't need all four of us to sell tickets. You can go home and work out some of the other logistics. We still need to confirm with the other bands, make sure all of the equipment is being delivered and all of that stuff. That way, you won't have to do anything you're uncomfortable with."

The rest of the group approved and waited for Annie's response.

"Well, okay, I guess that's fine," said Annie, reluctantly. Annie started to pick up her things and got ready to go. She did so slowly as if waiting to articulate her thoughts, trying to decide if she should push the issue anymore. After a couple of minutes she muttered goodbye and left the student union.

Just as Annie was leaving, some freshman students walked into the student union toward the Helping Hands group.

The first girl to approach the table asked, "Hey, is this where we can buy raffle tickets to meet Gianna this weekend?"

"Sure is!" replied Travis.

"I'll take ten, please! I'm not taking any chances. I *really* want to meet her!"

The Helping Hands members looked at each other for just a second, and then Sofia started to count out ten tickets while Travis opened the cash box in case change was needed. And Miles said, "Ten raffle tickets to meet Gianna, coming right up!"

KEY TERMS

decision making

ethics

groupthink

inference errors

leadership

DISCUSSION QUESTIONS

1. What was at stake for the Helping Hands fundraising committee in this situation?

2. What challenges to decision-making effectiveness are evident in this case? Give examples. How did these influence the group's decision making?

3. What is groupthink? What evidence of groupthink did you see in this case?

4. How did the suggestion to lie get brought up initially? How did humor play a part, and why might a group member use humor in this kind of situation?

5. What roles do you see evident in this case? How did these roles contribute to or challenge the group's decision to lie?

6. How did Annie handle the group decision? Could she have done anything to convince them to be honest?

7. Are the characters portrayed here the "type" to lie? Why or why not? What individual traits and communication styles might make someone more or less prone to going along with a group's decision to lie?

8. What can other groups learn from Helping Hands' dilemma?

PART

Groups and Democracy

A SMALL DEMOCRATIC GROCERY CO-OP

John Gastil and Justin Reedy

Members of an employee-owned grocery co-op use principles of deliberative democracy to work toward consensus on important financial decisions.

On a Monday evening in Madison, Wisconsin, dozens of shoppers pass through the Mifflin Street Community Co-op.[1] As customers select and ring up their groceries for the week, many realize that they aren't shopping in a typical corporate-owned grocery store. The organic products for sale and consumer information posted around the store make that obvious. But the shoppers may not know that the Co-op is also the site of weekly group discussions in which the staff govern the store itself. The people who work in the store decide the products sold, the employee work schedules, their professional development plans, and even how the store will aid political causes and local charities.

Upstairs from the sales floor, the staff members of the Mifflin Street Co-op gather each Monday evening for their weekly meetings. Unlike most workplace gatherings, these meetings don't simply involve a manager passing along information about new corporate policies or telling employees about new goals set by people higher up in the organization.

Instead, the Co-op staff gather each week to decide how they want to run the store, going through a process of open discussion and democratic decision making. The nine staff members file into a meeting room, arranging their chairs and floor cushions in a rough circle in preparation for the group's discussion. Dan, the appointed facilitator, helps the group stay on task and work through the meeting's agenda. As items come up, one of the staff members takes the lead in introducing and explaining the topic at hand—such as whether the store should donate snacks and beverages to an upcoming community forum. Other staff members ask questions, probing for more detailed information about the question at hand.

---

[1]This case is adapted from John Gastil, *Democracy in Small Groups: Participation, Decision Making, and Communication* (Philadelphia, PA: New Society Publishers, 1993). Additional descriptive detail has been added and two composite characters have been created for dramatic purposes.

Eventually, some employees share their opinions on the topic. The group may start to build consensus for a decision, reaching a point at which the staff members realize they all agree on a course of action. Other times, the group might see that some members disagree with the majority view, and they can either choose to abandon the decision—not donating to the forum at all, for example—or they can ask those minority members to stand aside and let the group reach a near-unanimous decision.

After finishing their discussion on one topic, the staff move to the next item on the agenda. And so on they go, from week to week, coming together in this small group to decide how the grocery store will be run and how the Co-op will be part of the Madison community.

GROUP DISCUSSION AND DELIBERATIVE DEMOCRACY

The Mifflin Street Co-op is more than just a quirky grocery store and workplace. It is also a self-conscious role model for the community—an example of how a group of equals can come together to make collective decisions. One useful way to understand the group discussions in the Mifflin Street Co-op staff meetings is to analyze them through the lens of deliberative democracy, which encourages free and open discussion of ideas and options.

In a deliberative democracy, there are several ideals set forth to ensure a vibrant discussion in which everyone gets to participate in the decision-making process. All the participants should have equal standing in the group, for instance, and everyone should have adequate opportunities to speak up. People should be respectful of others in the discussion and be open to others' ideas and experiences. Discussions should help create a good base of information about the topic being discussed and should help the group consider what values are at stake—and how to prioritize competing values. Participants should talk about a range of possible solutions to the problem at hand, perhaps even brainstorming about new solutions. They may then weigh all the pros, cons, and trade-offs of each option, giving real consideration to others' solutions, rather than simply sticking with one's preferred solution. Finally, the group should then make the best decision possible, taking into account all the information that members have learned as part of the discussion.

Two of the Mifflin Street Co-op's discussions provide a glimpse of how groups can try to put deliberative democracy into practice in the real world. One of their discussions shows how the group tries to ensure that members have many opportunities to speak up, and another shows how the group members try to listen carefully to one another.

SPEAKING OPPORTUNITIES AND RESPONSIBILITIES

In this first discussion, the Co-op's staff members are discussing a request for a donation to a local cause. This topic came up often in the staff meetings, since the Mifflin Street Co-op had a well-known commitment to community causes and regularly donated excess revenue or store inventory to local organizations. To help the group decide how to prioritize these requests, staff members would share relevant information about the cause or donation request and try to make earnest, persuasive arguments to the group. In this case, the group was considering a request from a group protesting against the first Gulf War in the early 1990s. Dan, the meeting facilitator and veteran of the sixties counterculture movement, kicks off the discussion.

"The other donation request on the docket for tonight is the folks from Women's International League for Peace and Freedom [WILPF] are organizing an ad [protesting the Persian Gulf War] to go in the *Isthmus* that reads, 'How many lives per gallon?'" Dan says. "It only costs $5 to sign on, and after paying for the ad, the $5 goes to further efforts toward organizing for peace in the Persian Gulf."

Sam, a younger activist who shares the same progressive values as the other Co-op members adds, "Stephen came in from Press House with this originally and showed it to Amy and me, and Amy threw $5 into it. I did it for myself. Amy did it as a representative of DARE, I think. Um—"

"Yeah, I think it would be best for Mifflin—" Dan begins.

"Yeah," interjects Amy, the oldest—and usually the quietest—member of the group.

"Yeah, it's not going in for a while—" Sam says.

"Yeah, it's going in either next weekend or the following weekend, and the due date is tomorrow," adds Dan.

The youngest staff member, Laura, looks perplexed. She scratches her head and appears distracted. "Yeah, I'm sorry, what was it going into?"

"The *Isthmus*," Sam replies, referring to the local newspaper in Madison. "Is it going to be a full-page ad or a half-page ad?"

"I think it depends on how much money they get," says Dan. Kate, the most experienced and forceful member of the group, nods seriously. "Let's do it."

Thus begins a rapid back-and-forth conversation involving nearly the entire group, with people asking for clarification about the amount the Co-op can afford to give, which budgets that money should come from, the viability of the WILPF plan to take out an expensive newspaper ad, and whether the Co-op should instead donate to a different anti-war action. One staff member suggests giving $20 to $25 of support, but another balks at the amount.

Kate shakes her head and looks around the room. "Why so much, though? Because if they're gonna get an ad, maybe it would be better for us to wait and give a more concrete type of aid rather than this."

Dan, who has been playing the dual role of facilitator and note-taker, looks up. "I agree with that position," he says. "My feeling in general on ads is that I'd rather give twenty-five bucks to someone giving a teach-in."

Dan's suggestion would support a single event, an educational forum focused on this political issue (known as a teach-in), rather than being a single donation for an expensive ad campaign. After another member points out that leftover donations to WILPF would go toward such events, the staff seems more supportive of donating to the organization. Other questions and issues arise and are addressed by staff members, and then Louis, a staff member who had not previously spoken, suggests ending the discussion. Louis, the tallest member of the group, sits uncomfortably on the old wooden chairs in the meeting room. He sports a scruffy beard and wears a "US Out of America" button.

"Let's decide something and get on with this," Louis says, taking a drink from a Dos Equis beer bottle and looking at his watch in the same instant.

"Maybe ten bucks," suggests Sam.

"From marketing or advertising? Or . . ." asks Kate.

"Ten bucks from organizing and—" Dan says.

"Ten from staff?" suggests Kate.

"Five from staff," Laura counters.

"Five from staff," Kate says in agreement.

"Fifteen total," says Dan, concluding the discussion. "Sounds good to me."

CAREFUL LISTENING

Another important aspect of deliberative democracy is thoughtful listening—the careful consideration of what others in the group are saying. In this next example from the Mifflin Street Co-op, the staff talk about an employee retention plan that would give monetary incentives to longer-tenured staff members. Long-time staff member Louis struggles with this idea, because he sees cash bonuses as going against some of the Co-op's ideals. Just after Amy finished describing the cash bonus plans, Louis leads off the discussion.

"I think it stinks," Louis says with a snort.

Sam sighs but looks up at Louis with a patient expression. "Why does it stink?"

"Just, I don't know, this is bizarre . . ." Louis replies. "I guess that's not very descriptive."

"'Stinks,' 'bizarre' . . ." Sam says, pointing out the vagueness of Louis's concerns.

"Why, Louis?" Amy asks, looking up from the notepad on which she's been writing.

"I don't know, it just strikes me as kind of filling our pockets or something," says Louis.

"That's what we're here on this Earth to do," Kate says with heavy sarcasm in her voice, causing the rest of the group to laugh.

Sam looks around the room anxiously. "I don't know, I think—"

"I think the percentage—" Louis starts to say.

"Do you understand that—" Amy asks.

"I understand that, um—" Louis continues.

"It's assuming that the person becomes more valuable," Amy says. "Well not 'more valuable,' but—"

"More *experienced*," says Kate, the employee with the most years logged at the Co-op.

"You said it!" Louis says and looks around the room, nodding his head and reaching down for his half-empty bottle of Dos Equis. "There is an assumption that you will become more valuable or more effective in the store. It's an assumption . . ."

"Well, it costs a lot to keep retraining somebody to replace someone," says Amy.

"Yeah, but it doesn't cost *this* much more," says Louis.

Amy shakes her head and looks up again from her notepad. "But I don't think the whole thing is just a reward for how valuable this person is. I think—"

"It sure comes off that way," Louis says, pointing the mouth of his bottle toward Amy.

Amy frowns. "If I could finish what I'm saying, it's sort of recognizing that this is a very profitable business, and it doesn't need to be some kind of financial sacrifice for people to work here."

The junior member of the Co-op, Laura, speaks for the first time. "I also wanted to say that just because we work in a co-op doesn't mean that our work should be devalued."

"I never said that," Louis responds.

"But you said that getting money as a compensation for staying 'stinks,'" Laura says, making quote marks in the air. "I just think that if you're going to take this as a serious job—one you can stay at for a very long time and retire from—we need to change policy, because you can't really support yourself in your retirement on the money we make now."

At this point, the discussion shifts to possible alternatives for the proposed monetary incentive system, with other group members pressing Louis for suggestions about how he thinks the Co-op should compensate experienced staff members.

"Do you have an alternative, Louis?" asks Amy.

"I think some existing models . . . I don't know, I would have to look into it," says Louis. "I don't know, but I think there are existing models in the industry that . . ."

"Would you feel more comfortable if it were some kind of retirement package?" Laura asks.

"Yeah, that's an idea," Louis responds.

"You know, to me that's a great concern, not that I'm ready for retirement—" says Laura, blushing as she looks at her senior colleague, Amy.

"Yeah, okay, the thing that really affected me was that this was thrown at us, and this was the only thing that some of us could come up with," says Louis. "I feel like everybody's adopting it without looking at anything else, and it seemed like we were already passing this before we even got to discuss any other alternatives."

AT THE NEXT MEETING

The topic comes up again at the next staff meeting, and again the group presses Louis for alternatives to the proposed cash bonuses. Sam and Louis lead off the discussion with some good-natured banter, eliciting laughter from the rest of the group before the meeting turns more serious.

"Do you think that the staff should get any benefits aside from the ones we get now?" Sam asks. "Is any increase in our benefits package excessive in your mind?"

"No, not necessarily," Louis says.

"Okay," Sam says.

"I really have a problem with this," Louis continues. "I think there are other alternative benefits, such as a clothing allowance or paid vacation. I really have problems with percentage numbers because they're based on . . . I don't know."

"Additional paid vacation is a percentage, too, it's just in a different form," Kate points out. "I don't think that it's—"

"Right, but it's more tangible in my perspective," Louis says.

"But you just have different needs from other people," counters Kate. "I need money, I don't need vacation. And I think that money—"

"That's actually a very interesting point worth pursuing," says Dan. "Should you have a staggered amount of time that you can take off, whether paid or unpaid? That's an idea."

"Yeah, we'll have to remember that," says Louis. "I don't know, I just . . . It bothers me, and right now I don't really have a clear enough head to continue my opposition to these proposals."

The discussion goes on, and Louis and the rest of the group continue to struggle with this topic. The other group members still have trouble understanding Louis's position, as he struggles to explain his opposition to the rest of the group.

"I guess I'm not sure what the difference is between the existing proposals and adding another week's paid vacation after a certain amount of time, because to me—" Amy says.

"It's not that much different, no," Louis agrees.

"It's the same thing," says Amy. "It's only that we're calling it something different."

"Yeah," says Louis.

"And it's figured in the same way, too," Amy says. She reaches down for a spreadsheet she's made to illustrate the different policies but then decides to place it in her lap without showing it to the group.

"In a way, yeah," says Louis. "Again—"

"Exactly the same way. I don't see a difference," says Amy.

"Okay, let me clarify it," Louis says. "My objection is to how it's presented. It looks to me as kind of a strange animal when you compare it to everything else that we've done in the Co-op with regard to benefits. It just, just really strikes me as a weird monkey. So, I don't know, maybe we could sit together and come up with a balance of these two ideas, instead of asking me over and over to clarify this—"

Sam and Amy point out that Louis still hasn't made his objection to the incentive system clear to the group, and that it might be time to end the discussion. Closing off discussion might seem "harsh," Sam says, but it might be the best option.

"My harshness is that I'm losing patience with the discussion," Sam says, standing up to stretch his back. "It hasn't been going that long, but I can see it circling for another hour before it comes in for a landing. I don't want to discuss it indefinitely, because I just can't see where . . . Okay, I don't know what I'm saying, but I don't want to continue without any forward progress."

The discussion continues even more, however, and the group again seeks more clarification from Louis, and staff members suggest other possible compromise solutions. Finally, Laura repeats Sam's earlier concern about the discussion not going anywhere.

"It seems like our discussion goes in more and more and more circles, so I'm not sure if more time will yield more circles or if more time will yield an alternative—a truly viable alternative," Laura says.

"Why assume that it wouldn't?" Louis counters.

"Because we've been talking and talking and talking and going in circles to circles to circles," Laura argues, waving her right hand above her head in a circular motion. "So I can't see where our circles are going to spiral out, you know."

"Well, fine," Louis concludes. "So go. I mean, I'm not going to block the consensus if you want it. I mean, I'm just giving you an alternative, and I still feel uncomfortable with this plan. If people are so burdened by this process or they feel so certain that this is what they want, then go. I'm not holding you up."

Five minutes later, deliberation ends, and the group agrees to close the discussion to reach a decision. They vote to adopt one of the three proposals for giving monetary incentives to longtime employees. Louis continues to oppose the group's choice but agrees to accept the decision anyway. He could have chosen to "block consensus" with a single veto vote, but he instead opts to "stand aside" and let the incentive plan become Co-op policy.

KEY TERMS

consensus

conflict

decision making

democracy

group climate

leadership

listening

DISCUSSION QUESTIONS

1. Discuss speaking opportunities versus responsibilities in a small business like this that is run by its staff. What are their personal, professional, or civic responsibilities to themselves, each other, their customers, or their community? Do those relate to any obligations that they have as group members to participate during discussions?

2. In this case, what rights do the group members have as speakers, and how do they exercise those rights? How do we establish and protect equal opportunity to speak in groups?

3. How do we learn that we have those rights, and under what circumstances might we *not* have such rights? If a group has limited time, which is more important— ensuring each *person* has equal time to speak or that each *viewpoint* has equal time to be considered?

4. What obligations do we have, if any, to listen to one another? What speaking and listening responsibilities did the members of Mifflin Co-op have? Are those different from the ones you have in the small groups of which you are a part?

5. In the case presented above, what are signs of careful, patient, or respectful listening? What are signs of inattentive listening or ignoring what someone has said?

6. How does the group work toward consensus? What benefits and challenges of consensus decision making are evident in this case?

DEBATING HATING

The Response and Responsibility of a Student Government

Stephen P. Konieczka

A university student senate uses parliamentary procedure while deciding how to respond to hate speech in the student newspaper.

In 2005 I began my first term as a representative on the legislative council of the most powerful student government in the United States, the University of Colorado Student Union (UCSU).[1] I had been involved in student government in high school but that experience did not prepare me for the scale and responsibility of UCSU.

Founded in 1974, UCSU is a tripartite government consisting of an executive, a legislature, and a judiciary, similar to the U.S. federal government. Day-to-day operations of UCSU center around the Legislative Council, or "Leg Council," and the executive branch, a three-person team know as the "Tri-Exes." The judiciary, which meets rarely, serves only to rule on constitutional questions.

Like other legislative bodies, Leg Council's primary power lies in its control of a budget, in this case, the student fee budget. UCSU collects and distributes approximately $34 million annually from hundreds of dollars our thirty-five thousand students pay each semester. The money is used to support the student union, health and recreation centers, and a host of other critical pieces of the university's social and physical infrastructure. Leg Council's unprecedented authority over the student fee budget (and other matters) is checked by the Tri-Exes, who are nonvoting members of Leg Council and have the power to veto any actions by the council.

---

[1]This case blends details, including quotations, from actual events with a fictionalized narration. The narrator's thoughts and statement prior to the meeting discussed are fictitious. Although names have been changed, all other quotes and events are nonfiction. Slight editing of some direct quotes was done for narrative coherence.

Despite its authority and the impact it can have on campus services, student involvement with UCSU has been waning in recent years. Total votes cast in spring polling declined every year between 2005 and 2009, from 23 percent to 15 percent, and meetings of Leg Council are sparsely attended. One exception to the rule of low participation is the annual budget hearings, when large numbers gather to plead for their piece of the fiscal pie. Another exception is when a politically charged issue is brought to our attention. When a campus controversy arises, people look for UCSU to respond.

In 2007 I was elected president of Leg Council. During my term as president several political controversies occurred on campus. Below I recount one of these incidents by telling the story of how Leg Council responded when a for-credit student publication ran articles many considered racist.

STOP *THE PRESS!* A CONTROVERSY ARISES

It was a Monday morning in late February 2008 when I awoke to find my mailbox flooded with angry e-mails. *The Campus Press*, the School of Journalism and Mass Communication's student publication, had released an article reading, in part, "They hate us all, and I say it's time we started hating them back. It's time for war."[2] The war was to proceed in three phases throughout which people of Asian descent were to be hunted, tortured, and subjected to reeducation.

Written by a student notorious for his offensive commentaries, the article appeared one day after the same publication posted to their website a piece denigrating Hispanics.[3] Many of the messages in my inbox called on UCSU to "do something" about these "racist" pieces of "journalism." I sighed, knowing the issue would consume most of my week (if not more), at a time when I needed to be working on the budget. Looking at my calendar, I saw that I also had two exams the following week; couldn't forget about those. As I wondered how all this work would get done, another e-mail arrived. It was from Rachel, a Tri-Exe, who told me she planned to introduce a resolution condemning the articles at this week's Leg Council meeting. "Another long week ahead," I posted to my Facebook page after reading Rachel's e-mail.

In my role as president I have two responsibilities directly related to meetings of Leg Council. The first is to prepare the meeting agenda, basically collecting and organizing items sent to me by the Tri-Exes and council members. My second responsibility is to be the meeting facilitator. Late for my first class, I rushed out the door, making a note to put Rachel's resolution on the agenda for the Council's next meeting.

---

[2]Karson, M. (2008, February 18). If it's war the Asians want . . . . *Campus Press*. Retrieved from http://web.archive.org/web/20080225193757/http://www.thecampuspress.com/home/index.cfm?event=displayArticle&ustory_id=c07cea4a-0e65-4465-a9c4-17d6deb357e8

[3]Geary, L. E. (2008, February 17) No hablo ingles: Try speaking English, this is the United States. *Campus Press*. Retrieved from http://web.archive.org/web/20080219130219/ http://media.www.thecampuspress.com/media/storage/paper1098/news/2008/02/17/Opinion/No.Hablo.Ingles-3214624.shtml

ANOTHER WEEK, ANOTHER MEETING: UCSU CONVENES

UCSU meets weekly on Thursday evenings during the school year. Our "chamber" is a long, thin room in the student union overlooking an outdoor fountain area. Tables are arranged to form a large rectangle taking up three-quarters of the room. Leg Council officers and the Tri-Exes sit at opposite ends of the rectangle with senators and representatives occupying the long sides. A public seating area is located directly behind the Tri-Exes.

When I arrived for Thursday's meeting, I greeted our secretary, who records the meeting minutes, and looked around the room. The public seating area was filled, with people overflowing into the hallway. "See, they do know we exist," I joked with the secretary.

Leg Council uses *Robert's Rules of Order* to guide meeting discussion and voting. As president of the council I facilitate the meetings. In that role I am an impartial observer, intervening in the discussion only to record speaking turns (also called "keeping the stack"), acknowledge speakers when their turn arises (sometimes called "recognizing"), and to rule on questions of procedural order. During meetings I tend to recede into the background making few, if any, contributions to the debate.

Normally, I enjoy the role of facilitator, which keeps me out of tedious debates. Tonight, I secretly wished to relinquish the gavel and with it the role of facilitator. Throughout the week, as I learned more about the situation surrounding the publication of the articles, I had formed strong opinions about *The Campus Press*'s decision to publish them and what UCSU's response should be. However, to effectively lead the meeting I needed to push those opinions aside.

Around 7 p.m. I took up the gavel and called the meeting to order. We began, as we always do, with a public comment period, followed by reports and other regular business.

YOU SAY YOU WANT A RESOLUTION?

After our regular business was completed I recognized Rachel, who introduced her legislation, "A Resolution in Response to Racist Articles Published in the *Campus Press*."[4] Introductions of legislation are an opportunity for a bill or resolution's sponsor(s) to frame the issue their legislation addresses, point out significant aspects of the legislation, and to field general questions. Before getting into those matters, Rachel requested James and John, two people who helped draft the resolution, be seated as nonvoting members for the discussion. Asking the trio to avoid repeating each other, I granted the request and settled in to listen.

"Both of the articles reinforce racist stereotypes that have created quite a stir," Rachel argued. "People are angry. People feel threatened and marginalized. I think these articles, especially the article 'If it's War the Asians Want . . .' specifically incite violence." Rachel went on to describe how meetings with campus administrators, SJMC faculty, and *Campus Press* staff left the impression there was little understanding among *The Campus Press*

---

[4]UCSU 68LCR#5 (2008). Retrieved from http://castle.colorado.edu/frames.htm

editors that their actions were wrong. "The editors just constantly reassert that their intention was for the articles to be satire, not hate speech," she explained. In closing her introduction, Rachel noted, "In my opinion, it's really important that UCSU, which is meant to be representative of the student body, say something about this. I really encourage you to pass this resolution."

It wasn't just Rachel who felt that UCSU should say something about the articles. Earlier in the week the Board of Directors of the National Asian American Student Conference (NAASCon), released a letter imploring "anybody of conscience to condemn Mr. Karson and those who afforded him the platform to spread his words of hate."[5] Condemnation of the articles came from high in the university's administration as well. CU's Chancellor, Office of Diversity, and School of Mass Communication and Journalism (SJMC) had released statements distancing the university from the articles.[6]

Implying that UCSU should follow the lead of others, James, one of the nonvoting members seated for the evening, summarized the public outcry: "The resolution tonight is proposing that UCSU take a stand on this. Students have come out earlier tonight to express their concerns. It has gone national. The chancellor has expressed concern."

When the sponsors finished their introductions I asked the council members if there were any questions. The question period, as I had to remind one member, is not a time for proposing amendments, but for clarifying inquiries about the resolution as proposed.

Representative Charles asked the only question. "Do you guys intend to try to pass this as an emergency act?" he inquired. If it were proposed as an emergency act, we would vote on final passage of the resolution immediately, not after a second reading the following week, which was the normal process. Rachel responded that she thought emergency action would be a good idea. It was important for UCSU to take a stand on the issue quickly, she said. "Oftentimes," John added, "things get swept under the rug. We really need to act right away."

Yes, I thought, we don't want this to drag on. Next week's agenda is already packed.

INTERESTS AND IDENTITIES PERFORMED

"Are there any other questions for the sponsors of the resolution?" I asked the council. "Seeing none," I continued, "we'd be in line for a motion." A motion was made to

---

[5]National Asian American Student Conference. (2008, February 25). *NAASCon statement regarding Max Carson's "If it's war the Asians want . . ." opinion piece.* Retrieved from http://capa-mi.blogs.com/capami/2008/03/naascon-stateme.html

[6]Peterson, G. P. (2008, February 20). *A statement by University of Colorado Chancellor G.P. "Bud" Peterson regarding a student column in the University of Colorado Campus Press.* Retrieved from http://www.colorado.edu/news/r/ 537a10e44b68770c42ff1040aff5de90.html

Voakes, P. (2008, February 21). *Letter to faculty from School of Journalism and Mass Communication Dean Paul Voakes.* Retrieved from http://www.colorado.edu/news/ statements/campuspress/voakes022108.html

move the resolution to a second reading. I had just finished stating for the record that the motion was seconded, when Charles's voice cracked. "Whoa! Wait," he excitedly declared.

There was confusion and different opinions as to the type of approval the motion contained. Whether or not the resolution would be moved as an emergency act could wait, I thought, and ruled that we were in discussion on moving the resolution to a second reading. I recognized SJMC Senator Linda.

Linda opened by proposing two amendments, one that stated the articles were meant to be satire and another recognizing *The Campus Press*'s efforts to address problems leading to their publication. Linda explained her first amendment made clear the articles were meant to be satire. She hastily added, "It's not funny. I know it's not funny. It was really terrible. But that was the original intent." The second amendment, Linda said, showed "*Campus Press* is working to address the concerns people have raised. We need to acknowledge that."

"Is there a second on the amendment?" I asked. The amendment was seconded, and we moved to a separate list of speakers regarding the amendment. I now had two stacks to manage—one on the resolution in general and one for Linda's amendment. Later in the evening, as amendments were made to amendments, managing these multiple stacks would prove difficult. For the moment, things were simple, and we entered discussion on the amendment, which was passed by acclimation after only one question.

"We'll move back to the main speakers list regarding the motion as a whole," I explained, reminding council members where we were in the process. "Senator Oscar," I said, giving him the floor.

"I'm going to really try . . ." Oscar hesitatingly began. "If I do cry, it's because of sadness, it's because of frustration and anger."

That got everyone's attention. The eyes of council members, usually affixed on laptops and cell phones, all turned to Oscar. He continued, "Time and time again this campus has been hit with racial issues and I don't understand why there's nothing in place to stop it." By the time Oscar had finished speaking he was in tears and left the room, followed by another council member seeking to console him.

FREEDOM OF SPEECH FOR WHOM?

Oscar's emotional reaction to the topic left stillness in the room, which I broke by slowly saying we would move to Representative Brian.

Brian proposed an amendment to remove the words "target" and "marginalized" from the resolution. As he explained, "While it might be a small thing, those two—to target and to put somebody down—while it's not moral, and it's wrong, and I disagree with it; it is unfortunately protected by freedom of speech. The parts that are not protected are to threaten and to incite violence against."

In this manner we broached a topic that would occupy much of our time, specifically the relationship between Leg Council and the First Amendment to the U.S. Constitution. I recognized Representative Dennis, the council's vice president.

"We value First Amendment freedom of speech," Dennis said. "But there's also a right of people to have their freedom to be safe. I think the resolution needs to reflect that because the intent doesn't matter. What matters is the impact. That's what people live with."

"We'll move on to Representative Charles," I instructed.

Charles used his turn to argue that the resolution should reflect the importance of the First Amendment issues in question. Summarizing, Charles explained, "While this particular situation falls under that [unprotected class of speech] there are many other situations that also fall under freedom of speech that should be protected. I don't want to get everything else caught up in this situation."

Moving down the stack, Diana, a Tri-executive, was next in line. Returning to Dennis's point, Diana explained the article "had a big enough impact that someone had to walk out of the room. I think that speaks very loudly to the actual impact of the article. . . . Yes, freedom of speech is something that we value in this country. However, when it makes people feel this way and when it is in a threatening way that is not satirical, it's not funny. It's wrong on many different levels."

Discussion of Brian's amendment continued for several turns on the same themes until Dennis was recognized again. He told the council, "We honor their [the authors' and *The Campus Press*'s] freedom of speech, but that shouldn't limit our ability to exercise our freedom of speech. We have every right as students, as a voting body, as a legislative body, to say we don't support this. I'd encourage voting down this amendment right now and I call the question."

PROCEDURES, RULES, AND ORDER, OH MY!

To "call the question" is a technical way of saying, "Let's vote." A vote, however, cannot be taken until the motion is seconded. Dennis's motion to vote was seconded but before we could proceed, Brain asked if he could withdraw the amendment.

I'd prefer we vote, I explained, calling for a show of hands. Not one was raised in support.

We moved on to Rachel, who had an amendment similar to Brian's. Oddly, the same course of events played out. After a brief discussion, the question was called and Rachel, out of turn, exclaimed, "I'll just retract it."

The deliberation that takes place during discussion is meant to make a bill stronger through amendments and make amendments as good as they can be through debate. Our discussion on Rachel's and Brian's amendments convinced them that neither would pass so they attempted to avoid the vote. Both Brian and Rachel, however, were long-time members of UCSU (Brian would succeed me as Leg Council president). They should have known that according to *Robert's Rules*, an amendment cannot be retracted. I chalked up their lapses to the fact that we had been discussing the resolution for about fifty minutes. It was now 9 o'clock on a Thursday just before midterm exams; people, including myself, were growing weary.

Attempting to maintain an orderly process, I informed Rachel that she could not retract the amendment. Her motion failed to gain support, and we moved back to the main speaker list. Yet we were soon back into the realm of procedural questions.

Dennis sparked this round by asking whether the original motion to move to second reading meant that to pass the resolution as an emergency act required voting the motion down and then reintroducing the resolution. I looked confusedly at Dennis, trying to wrap my head around his question. I soon realized he was basically asking how we would proceed to the final vote.

"The way we would do this," I responded, "is the resolution would have to be voted down and another motion would be made. There are three other motions that could be made. They are to table the resolution, pass it special order, or refer it to committee."

"Does that include Linda's amendments or just the original?" Senator Eric inquired.

No amendment had been made, I reminded the senator, a misstatement met with protests all around. I had failed to record Linda's amendments, which were approved early in the meeting. I paused the meeting to make the correction and told the council any vote, emergency or otherwise, would be on the amended resolution.

"Mr. President," I heard Linda say as I made the correction, "I move that we suspend the bylaws in order to effectively and efficiently address this issue." This declaration, another turn and proposal made out of order, opened the door for others to begin speaking out of turn. The clamor grew quite loud.

Perhaps we should have dealt with the issue of second reading verses emergency action earlier, when the council was less fatigued, I thought. Too late now. Taking a deep breath, I quieted everyone and explained how we would proceed.

"This is the way this is going to work," I stated. "We're in discussion. We could call it to question and vote it down. If we wanna go to an emergency act we'd have to repropose the motion to pass an emergency act. That would open up another discussion. We'd be at the same point, but it'd be under the line item of an emergency action." We continued with our deliberations for a few minutes, until Charles called for a vote to move the resolution to second reading.

"I object," a council member exclaimed. This objection required a vote on Charles's motion to vote. By roll call, in which each member of the council stated their preference for the record, the motion to move to second reading failed on a vote of 6 to 11.

It is worth noting that although I thought emergency action was appropriate, Charles's request for a second reading was an equally sensible position. As he said, "This is something that has been an issue for a while. . . . I t is a constant issue that we are battling. I don't see why it should be treated as an emergency."

Thinking about Charles's position, I recognized Dennis, who made a motion to pass the resolution as an emergency act. The motion was seconded and we entered another discussion phase.

During the discussion a final amendment was proposed, which the council agreed through acclimation to adopt. After the vote, and before I could finish saying that we would return to the stack, Charles hollered: "Call the question." The motion was seconded, and after more than seventy minutes of deliberation and procedural complications, the resolution, with two amendments, passed without objection as an emergency act.

KEY TERMS

decision making

ethics

facilitation

group structure

roles

leadership

task and relational communication

DISCUSSION QUESTIONS

1. The story's narrator explained that to effectively lead the meeting he needed to push aside his opinions. Why would he feel the need to do this? How do you think it helped or hindered his ability to facilitate the meeting?

2. Do you think the narrator did a good job of facilitating the meeting? What could he have done better?

3. Keeping a stack, or list of speakers, is commonplace in meetings of this type. How do you think the stack structured the discussion? In what ways did the stack help or hinder the discussion?

4. *Robert's Rules of Order* is only one way a meeting can be facilitated. What other facilitation procedures do you think could have been used to manage UCSU's discussion? What type of group facilitation would you not propose for this group?

5. Rachel requested that two people join the Council for the meeting discussed in this case. When should groups involve non-members in their discussion? What are the costs and benefits of having non-members participate in a group's discussion?

6. What kind of evidence did group members use to support their arguments? How much influence did these different types of evidence have on the discussion?

7. Linda was the senator from the School of Journalism and Mass Communication, meaning she represented the School's interests in the meeting. How did her amendment represent the School's interests?

8. Towards the end of their deliberations, the group experienced a lot of confusion regarding procedures. What would you suggest the group do to avoid such confusion in the future?

A Different Kind of Public Meeting

Engaging a Public Controversy through Small Groups

Martín Carcasson and Leah M. Sprain

A school board official uses small group facilitators to engage parents in a successful discussion about proposed changes to the local schools.

As the director of communication for the school district, I am responsible for managing the relationships between the district and parents, teachers, and students.[1] Basically, I am in charge of public relations, connecting the school district with the community. When controversial decisions need to be made, I'm often responsible for responding to angry e-mails and phone calls or working with the local newspapers to share information about what is happening. In the spring of 2007, our district took on a tough issue, one that I feared would raise a lot of concern and rancor within the district.

Our district was one of the few districts in Colorado to be configured with elementary schools housing kindergarten to sixth grade, junior highs ranging from seventh to ninth grade, and three-year high schools. Most of the state utilized K–5, 6–8, and 9–12 configurations. The primary concern for the district was the ninth graders currently in junior highs. Smaller junior highs offered a more limited curriculum and fewer extracurricular activities, which we worried was a disadvantage to students, especially since their ninth-grade year counted on their applications toward college. Ninth graders were also allowed to participate in varsity sports at the high schools, which caused a variety of logistical problems. But many parents liked the fact that their younger children stayed in elementary school as long as possible, essentially extending their childhood one extra year. A committee made up of

---

[1]This case is based on a real set of public meetings run by the Center for Public Deliberation. The first author (Martín) helped organize and run these meetings. Although grounded in real events, the dialogue and voice of the narrator (the school district director of communication) are fictionalized accounts. None of the material in this case study should be attributed to actual people. Aside from Martín, all the names in this case study are pseudonyms.

district officials, parents, and community members had been studying the issue for a while and were nearing a decision. Before they made a recommendation to the school board, however, we needed to provide the public with an opportunity to weigh in on the issue.

I knew that it was a controversial issue. Some parents didn't even want to consider making a change, particularly because the district was currently performing so well. Other parents saw more opportunities for their kids if we switched systems. I really wanted to engage the public in a productive way, but I worried that the usual sort of public hearing would likely be unproductive in this situation and primarily highlight the loudest voices. With such strong divides, how could we get public input without further dividing public opinion?

I decided to contact Colorado State University's Center for Public Deliberation (CPD). Meeting with Professor Martín Carcasson, we discussed that typical public hearings primarily involve individuals getting a chance to express themselves—often at a microphone in front of a large crowd—but offer little opportunity for actual interaction between participants or even between participants and institutional decision-makers. I knew we wanted more interaction between participants so we could move beyond hearing prepared statements and actually have people learn from each other and refine their positions. We also knew that some parents didn't trust the school district and would be looking for opportunities to express their frustration. Martín said this distrust was a good reason to have a neutral third party run the process. In fact, he had a group of students who were trained to help run meetings for situations just like this.

At the CPD, undergraduate students were trained to be designers, facilitators, and reporters of public forums and ran a variety of events in the local community. The students had specific training to facilitate small group discussions about difficult public policy issues. They learned how to ask good questions, paraphrase, and handle situations such as people being too emotional, confrontational, or simply dominating the conversation, as well as how to capture the discussions on easels in plain view of the participants. Overall, they worked to help the groups be more civil and productive and to make sure the issue was considered broadly and fairly.

I decided to work with Martín and have the CPD students help convene the meetings. Together we developed a plan. We developed background material on the issue, including four different ways that the district could approach the issue. A handout would be given to all participants that listed these different approaches and outlined arguments for and against each one. Each meeting would start with thirty minutes of background information on grade reconfiguration. After this introduction, participants would be split into small groups with a focus on getting people to talk to each other. A CPD facilitator would work with a group of ten to twenty-five parents to discuss what they liked and didn't like about each of these four possible approaches to the issue. In going through each of these approaches, the purpose wasn't to vote on which one to select. Instead, the discussion was designed to have people explain their appreciations and concerns for each of the approaches in order to get a full sense of all the possibilities and drawbacks. As participants started talking to one another, the hope was they would be able to identify and weigh the competing reasons to address grade configuration, realizing that no approach was perfect and that difficult trade-offs were inevitable. Ideally, participants would better understand what was at stake in making this decision while also sharing their perspectives and reasons with the district.

As Martin and I talked, I got excited about this approach. But I wasn't quite sure how parents would respond to this different format for a public meeting. Would they get angry? Would they like being in small groups, or would they miss having a microphone in their hand and getting to command the attention of the entire crowd? Would they listen to each other? Would the CPD student facilitators be able to handle any potential outbursts?

After watching one group at the first meeting, I knew we had made the right choice. Our plan provided parents with an opportunity to voice their concerns and hear different opinions. Not only did the district get good information to help inform our decision, parents seemed to really listen to one another and understand different opinions. Watching the small groups, I realized that this was a different way—a better way—to involve the public in key school direct decisions.

Let me describe one of the many small group discussions that occurred during the six public meetings we held.

Each classroom used for the small group discussions had chairs set up in a semicircle facing two easels. A student facilitator from the CPD, Mallorie in this particular room, sat in the open end of the circle, while additional students (Sara and Jack) took notes on the easels. The small group time was designed to have each group first discuss why they came to the forum—to better understand their motivations and the values they brought to the issue—followed by dedicated time to discuss each of the four potential approaches.

Once the fifteen participants were seated in the semicircle, the students introduced themselves. Mallorie explained, "My name is Mallorie, and I'm a student at Colorado State University. Today my role is to help facilitate this discussion about grade configuration. My role is to help guide us through each of the different approaches that are outlined on in your information packet, to hear your appreciations and concerns for each of these approaches to addressing grade configuration. As much as possible, this time is designed to have you talk to each other. I just want to review a few ground rules that we have in place to make sure that this is a safe space for everyone to contribute. The ground rules are posted here on the wall:

- The goal is to help make the best decision for the community as a whole.

- Speak honestly and respectfully.

- Listen carefully and respectfully.

- One person talks at a time.

- Be brief to allow all to participate.

"My role is to help make sure that everyone who wants to speak has the opportunity to express their opinions. Sara and Jack will be taking notes of your comments so that we can share those with the district. Every word they write will be typed up and included in the report we provide the district, which will be posted on the website. Keep in mind that we're impartial—our job is to fairly run the process. If you don't think that we've accurately captured your comment, please let us know. We want to make sure that your thoughts are being captured accurately."

As Mallorie presented the ground rules, most of the parents listened intently, looking over to the rules posted on the walls. A few parents seemed more on edge as though they were eager to voice their opinions; they shifted a bit in their seats and whispered side comments to people sitting next to them during the introduction.

"To start, let's hear why this issue is important to you. Why did you come tonight?"

"I'll start," said Sabrina Togelson, a parent of a fifth grader. "I came tonight because I'm really concerned about this talk that my daughter might be moved into a middle school without having the chance to be a leader at her elementary school. She's been waiting for so long for the opportunity to be at the top of the school and that will be taken away. Plus I don't like the idea of her being around older kids. I guess I think that elementary school is such an important place for a child, and I want my daughter to be able to stay there as long as possible."

"I'm a teacher at Boltz, a local junior high," said Tim Williams. "This decision will impact my curriculum and the classes that I teach. No matter the approach, this decision will have a big impact on teachers in the district. Obviously, I'm concerned about the education for our students, but I'm here tonight to make sure that teacher perspectives are included in the discussion."

"I also have two kids in the district. I've heard a lot of rumors about possible grade changes—it seems like the district may have already made a decision. I'm here tonight because I want to know more about what is going on," said Keelie James.

"Obviously, this issue impacts everyone in this room, perhaps in different ways," Mallorie explained. "The process tonight is designed to hear from all of you as we talk through different approaches to addressing this topic. As I said before, we aren't going to vote on which one you like best, but I do want to discuss the benefits and problems with each of these approaches. Some of the arguments for and against each of the approaches are listed in the background information. Feel free to express one of these arguments or offer your own comments as to your reaction to this approach. Let's start with Approach A, which is to maintain the current grade configuration. What do you like about this option?"

"Well, if it isn't broken, it doesn't need to be fixed. Seriously, our district has such great schools. I don't understand why we would mess with a system that seems to be working. I'm in favor of just keeping everything the same," said Kyle Jones, a parent of three students.

"Building on that, this system seems to work really well for sixth graders who get to be leaders in their elementary schools. We shouldn't rush sixth graders to develop and mature any faster than they already do. I guess I feel like there is a whole lot less pressure on them in elementary school than there would be in a junior high," added parent Stephanie Garcia.

Sabrina Togelson interjected, "Yeah, let sixth graders remain kids."

Mallorie noted, "So several people have said that they like the current system because it allows sixth graders to remain in elementary schools where they can flourish. How do other people feel about this argument?"

Darrie Michaels replied, "Well, most of the other districts in Colorado have sixth graders in middle schools, and they don't seem to be having problems. I guess I'm not convinced that sixth graders won't be able to handle the transition. But my real concern is for ninth graders. It seems like ninth graders really need the opportunities that are available in high schools that aren't available in junior highs. I want my kids to be able to take advanced classes, participate in sports, etc. Keeping them back in junior high for another year puts them at a competitive disadvantage to kids from all the other districts across the state."

"So, I hear you voicing a concern about Approach A that it isn't good for ninth graders because they don't have as many opportunities? Is that accurate?" asked Mallorie.

"Exactly," said Darrie.

"I don't see it," remarked Yesmin Plakka. "I think that the superintendent is just trying to make a name for himself so that he gets more money or a better job somewhere else. The whole thing just seems trumped up. We don't need to change. They've never really explained why we need to have this conversation at all and consider such a drastic change. The superintendent is pushing this agenda through. He's on a power trip, and no one really cares what we think at all."

Sabrina replied, "You know I don't want to change the grades, and personally I'm not so sure about the superintendent either. But hearing Darrie I've realized that there are other parents who want to have this conversation and are frustrated with the limitations of the current configuration. And just because it's working well now doesn't mean it couldn't work even better. Maybe it isn't just the district pushing an agenda."

"I'm actually concerned about opportunities for ninth graders too," added Jill Mitchell. "Right now I teach ninth graders in junior high. I have a hard time reminding students to take their grades seriously. Even though they attend a junior high, their grades count toward college applications. Too many of our students don't realize that getting a B- or C+ or D matters. I feel as though being in a high school setting would help raise the stakes a bit. At the same time, they would be able to make the most of so many opportunities that aren't available in our junior highs. I feel as though the current system delays a transition that would be good for students. Keep in mind—I'm a teacher. I might have to move buildings, to change my classes. Personally, I don't really want to do that. But I really do think that some of my students—particularly those that are college-bound and want to take harder classes—would benefit from being in a high school."

"But what about other students? Those who aren't going to be taking honors classes?" probed Kyle Jones.

"Well, I think that the transition could be good for them too. Our high schools offer a variety of vocational opportunities that could be a better fit for these students. The variety of opportunities at high school is simply larger. This would benefit all students, not just athletes or A students," replied Jill.

"I'm not sure that I agree. In high school there are more opportunities, including opportunities to get in trouble or fall into the wrong crowd. I feel like ninth graders aren't ready to make good and appropriate decisions regarding drugs, alcohol, and tobacco," said Kyle. "Having a closed campus at junior high means that there is simply less opportunity for those sort of bad choices. Right now ninth graders get to be role models. I'm afraid that moving them would mean that students would try to impress older students by trying to fit in. We all know that peer pressure makes kids make stupid decisions."

"I don't think we should change," interjected parent Tina Key.

"Why is that?" probed Mallorie.

"Well, it seems like my kids are eager to grow up so fast already. They want to watch PG-13 movies and hang out with their friends without me around. My daughter wants to wear makeup—I fear she'll want to wear shorter and shorter skirts. I guess I worry that these tendencies will be even worse if we change the grade configuration. It would be like sending a message that we consider you older. I don't want my kid to grow up any faster; I don't want the school district telling her that she's older than she is."

"Yeah," responded Jill. "My own daughter is a freshman in college. I understand how you feel. But I'm not sure that changing the grade configuration would really be sending your daughter the message that she should be reckless in any of the ways that you fear. Instead, the kids in my class often rise to the occasion. I think that your daughter might be able to develop emotionally in a setting where she is challenged. I'm not so quick to be sure that this change would automatically be bad for kids. But I understand why parents are cautious."

Mallorie noted, "We're nearing the end of our time to focus on Approach A. Are there any additional comments, perhaps from someone who hasn't yet had a chance to speak, about Approach A?"

"I guess . . ." started Al Yanka, a parent and teacher in the district. "I guess I can see this issue from both sides, as a parent and teacher. And from both of these sides, I don't think that there is a clear direction. I agree that we have great schools. And I understand why some parents hesitate to change anything because we all want our kids to be in safe and high-performing schools. But at the same time, I really see some cool opportunities for our kids if we consider changing. I guess I want to at least be open to exploring other ways of doing things. But I'm cautious too. I wouldn't want to do anything that would make things worse for my kids—the ones in my classroom or the ones who live in my house."

"That's actually a nice transition to begin to talk about Approach B," said Mallorie.

Mallorie continued to walk the group through each of the different approaches. As the director of communication, I couldn't help but be impressed by the level of conversation that people were having. For the most part, people were explaining their reasons behind preferences and seemed to understand some of the reasons why other parents or teachers disagreed with them.

At the end of each meeting, after the participants had walked through all the approaches and the walls of the classroom were filled with the notes from the discussion, the participants were provided with five small dot stickers and instructed to place the dots next to the statements on the notes with which they most agreed. This provided all the participants with the opportunity to review all the comments that had been made during the evening and furnished the district with a better sense of the overall support for various arguments.

At the end of all of the meetings, Martin compiled a report that included all the comments—every single comment written down by a note-taker—and identified central themes. The dot process allowed him to show which appreciations and concerns were most important to those who particiated. These were the perspectives that we needed to consider both in our decision as well as in how we would implement that decision. In the end, the district decided to make the change, moving the sixth and ninth graders up. We did postpone it for a year, partly due to public input from the forums that had expressed concern about the district's preparedness for the change. Other concerns we heard impacted how we enacted the change.

When the change occurred in the fall of 2009, it went remarkably smoothly. Braced for a slew of angry e-mails and phone calls from concerned parents and frustrated school staff, I heard almost nothing. In fact, a local newspaper reporter said that they too were expecting to report on the conflict over grade configuration, only to find no controversy. I couldn't help but smile. Using small group discussions with trained, impartial facilitators to work through this issue was a much better plan than holding typical public meetings.

KEY TERMS

facilitation

meeting management

leadership

listening

problem solving

DISCUSSION QUESTIONS

1. How did this meeting differ from a more typical public hearing? Why did the narrator feel that a deliberative discussion was a better way to approach this issue?

2. What strategies did Mallorie use to structure this meeting? How did her facilitation choices and use of guidelines influence the way the discussion went?

3. What were the key issues at stake for the people who participated in the meeting? Describe the problem-solving approach used in this group. How were the issues communicated about in the group?

4. How would you describe the group members' listening in this case? Give an example of the listening behavior exhibited by group members. How did this listening influence the group's climate and its ability to discuss the issue?

5. How did this group discussion influence the final decision made by school district?

6. How would you describe Mallorie's leadership? Why do you think she decided to lead the group in the way she did? What would happen if she used a different leadership strategy?

7. What can other groups learn about facilitation, problem solving, and deliberation from this case?

REBUILDING COMMUNITIES WITH THE PUBLIC SQUARE PROCESS

Timothy Steffensmeier and Terry Woodbury

A community leader helps people develop civic leadership skills by facilitating citizen discussions about challenging community issues.

PUBLIC SQUARE PROCESS: A COMMUNITY CONVERSATION

Terry Woodbury, a white-haired man with a knack for conversation, is standing in front of eighty-five citizens in a rural Kansas county. Residents have gathered in a large metal building that doubles as a site for county fair activities and community festivities. For most people gathered tonight, the agenda for this community-wide conversation is unknown. And it is likely that many in attendance are skeptical of this outsider who claims to be in the business of rebuilding communities. Over the past three decades, consultants and economic developers have come to this community promising jobs and prosperity and have left only to have perpetuated the population decline that has afflicted most U.S. rural communities. With a steady confidence and melodious voice, Terry begins the community conversation by pointing to a hand-drawn sign and reading: "Positive Conversation Changes the World." Most people speak a statement like this and sound at best clichéd or at worst naïve, particularly when a community's survival is on the line. Yet tonight the words resonate. Terry speaks these words genuinely as lessons learned from education in a one-room country school and a Princeton seminary; then eighteen years of revitalizing a four-by-four-block urban neighborhood and presiding over a United Way board.

So here is Terry in his latest role as founder and president of Public Square Communities, LLC, teaching civic skills with a process that grew organically from urban and rural life experiences. Terry provides more details: "Each time we gather together to discuss the future of this community, we need to include people from all four sectors of the public square," and he gestures to another handwritten poster with four quadrants labeled as (1) Human Service, (2) Government, (3) Business, and (4) Education. He explains: "When people from each sector of the public square are present in a discussion, it will help ensure that the community's agenda is being surfaced and not that of a particular institution or one sector of the public square." Terry asks the group to begin rebuilding their community by "talking differently." For the people gathered this evening, this new conversation will become the glue for making progress on their hopes for this place.

I am listening from the back of the room as a researcher, primarily there to collect data for a book on civic deliberation. And I am smiling because this seemingly democratic process is grounded in communication, and it is becoming clear that this is not a lecture or sage-on-the-stage event. Terry Woodbury is modeling and facilitating a distinct form of civic conversation.

After the introduction of the Public Square process, Terry charges small groups of seven to ten people to discuss their hopes for the community. The citizens begin talking to one another about the issues they care most about. After everyone at the table has had an opportunity to share, members from each group report to the large group on a hope that they heard at their table. One citizen talks about wanting a place for seniors to gather. A middle-aged woman states her hope that job opportunities will be created so her college-bound children can return to a place they love. And a teenager reiterates a desire to stick around if there were only good work to be had. The most telling moment comes from a woman in her mid-thirties who gave this passionate plea: "I hope the negative talk and divisive actions in this community are replaced with optimism and people coming together to work on the same page." Many heads nodded in response as this community has been experiencing a decade-long conflict regarding a hospital issue that has left many residents feeling divided. Terry pipes up and labels this chronically negative talk as the "cancer in the coffee shop." Communities tend to have a place, Terry explains, where people convene to tell and retell all that is wrong with the town without ever taking action to produces better results.

After community members share their hopes, I present data to the group from forty interviews we conducted in the community. During these one-on-one interviews with citizens from all four sectors of the public square, we asked residents to identify community resources that are primary determinants of youths' success. After explaining the data results, I ask each small group to discuss how the community could use its two strongest youth resources to enhance a low-performing resource. The groups dialogue to invent strategies and commit their ideas to paper. I collect the written suggestions and report on the strategies to the entire group.

Later during this three-hour community conversation, Terry and I introduce civic engagement stories that we had been told during our interviews of community residents. One story describes the renovation of a park that had been initiated by a small group of citizens, including a teacher, business owner, elected official, and health care worker. Terry emphasizes that this is civic engagement because people were working across the four sectors of the public square to make progress on a collective issue. The park's success is attributed, in part, to a small group of people who bridged sectors of the public square to accomplish their task. After sharing stories of civic engagement, the small groups are asked to recall instances of civic engagement and develop ways to improve upon those successes to address contemporary needs.

At the end of this initial community conversation, citizens are asked to nominate people for the next phase of the Public Square process, a visioning retreat. Terry encourages people to nominate bridge builders—those residents who have the capacity to work across sectors of the public square. He also asks that unlikely participants be considered for the visioning process. At a day-long visioning meeting, some fifty people will gather to create a vision statement and determine action teams who will address needs that were developed during the conversation tonight. And with that, the first community conversation concludes. Many people approach Terry and me to comment on how good it felt to discus with peers their hopes for the future. There is also a hint of optimism that this process could turn the page on long-standing divisive issues. As we pack up our belongings, I reveal to Terry that tonight had reshaped my connection to this work. Standing on the sidelines and writing about this work is not the best use of my communication skills. It is time to engage with Public Square Communities in a more direct manner.

PUBLIC SQUARE PROCESS: CONVENING THE STEERING COMMITTEE

The community meeting just described illustrates a typical community conversation that begins this multiyear Public Square process. In these meetings, community members engage in small group and large group discussions that help create a vision for the community development process. The Public Square process is made possible by particular structural components, communication processes, and leadership acts. One example of a small group that is essential in the Public Square process is a citizen-driven *steering committee*. Typically six to twelve members serve on a community's steering committee, which operates as a freestanding group at the center of the public square. The steering committee is not an official board or an arm of an institution (e.g., chamber of commerce), and it lacks formal authority to act in any given sector of the public square. To illustrate the inner workings of this small group, we turn to Gary and Jesse, two citizen participants of the Public Square process who are co-conveners of their community's steering committee.

Gary and Jesse—a middle-aged proprietor of a bed and breakfast inn and a young loan officer at a family-owned bank—are conveners working to improve public conversation. Both are busy at their jobs; yet they make time to volunteer for civic causes, one of which is the community's Public Square steering committee. The steering committee that Gary and Jesse serve on includes between eight and twelve people from four sectors of the community—business, education, government, and human services. This diverse group guides the Public Square process by organizing *community conversations* (described above) and *vision retreats* to establish community goals. In addition, the steering committee coordinates and sustains several volunteer citizen groups called action teams. These *action teams* work to achieve a community goal.

Gary and Jesse are tasked with bringing people together to clearly identify and overcome a community problem. In other words, they convene diverse groups of people to make better decisions on their most pressing public issues. The public square serves as both a material and metaphorical starting point for these conveners because rebuilding "community" is not exclusively about renovating buildings or starting new businesses downtown. It is also about rebuilding social cohesion: replacing separation, distrust, and vitriolic criticism with cooperation, trust, and positive conversation.

Gary and Jesse address these needs as co-conveners of a steering committee located in a rural county with a population estimated at three thousand people. Together they set the meeting's agenda; then, one or both of them facilitate a monthly two-hour steering committee meeting. In this particular community, the initial community-wide conversation and vision retreat created the following goals: (1) revitalizing a large public park to become a regional recreation facility, (2) recruiting and coordinating volunteers to take on local cleanup and improvement projects, (3) maximizing the use of existing public facilities and local talent to attract regional traffic, (4) developing youth leaders to become involved civically and attach to the community in a way that may influence them to return in the future, and (5) developing the airport to better serve local businesses and tourism.

An action team comprised of a small group of citizen volunteers addresses each of the goals outlined above. With steering committee support, the action teams have been reasonably successful. Volunteer efforts improved the appearance and design of a park to include a new walking trail and Frisbee golf course. Another action team engaged youth to participate in making a promotional YouTube video to attract new residents. Meanwhile the steering committee began to play an important mediatory role for community conflicts.

Jesse and Gary's civic leadership style enables the steering committee to emerge as a credible convener of disparate groups who are accomplishing these goals for the larger community good. On four separate occasions over a two-year period, the steering committee has inserted itself into a conflict and, in each case, helped the community turn trouble into opportunity.

Overcoming Conflict at the Park

Developing the park was the first community project. Because park development was a Public Square goal and had an action team leading the way, the project activated lots of volunteer attention. Despite a high level of involvement from established volunteer groups and positive energy around the project, trouble began to brew because each group had different leadership styles and agendas. These differences collided at the park. Furthermore, the city—which owned the park—was complicit in the emerging conflict because it was happy to let volunteers do all the work, even though the group members were fighting with each other, getting burned out, and becoming angry with the city maintenance crew for sitting idly by.

With tensions rising, the steering committee intervened by calling for a meeting of representatives from all stakeholders in the park. The meeting included these groups: Pheasants Forever, the golf course, the city, the Gun Club, and a couple of lesser players. A neutral facilitator from Public Square Communities was asked to facilitate the meeting of about twenty-five citizens. After a three-hour facilitated conversation, a task force of stakeholder groups had been named, a trusted individual had been chosen to moderate future meetings, and a timeline for task completion had been developed. A month later, responsibilities and roles were clarified and a coordinated team effort was moving forward.

Forming a Workable Chamber and Economic Development Relationship

For several years, the Chamber of Commerce and Economic Development organizations shared the same building with offices about twenty feet apart. The chamber ran on a thin budget and part-time staff supported by chamber dues and augmented by volunteers. Economic Development had a full-time director supported by taxes. The organizational styles of these two groups were quite distinct, and the personalities of the directors were like oil and water. One director was full-time, quite autonomous, and displayed a kind of brusque authority. The other director was part-time, more an executive assistant than a director, who had a limited scope of work and very modest pay. This person seemed victimized by expectations beyond her abilities to handle. For these reasons, the two offices and organizations coexisted at best and avoided each other where possible.

Again, the public square—urged by co-conveners Gary and Jesse—intervened. Public Square Communities was called upon to serve as a neutral facilitator for the meeting. With volunteers from the chamber and the board of directors for Economic Development, the group was smaller than the public conversation on the park project. The group size allowed for a more intimate and direct conversation. During the conversation, a plan was ironed out so that both groups could contribute to large community promotion projects. In addition, a communication system was created to nourish a dialogue between the groups.

Responding to Community Opposition Over Airport Development

The airport action team, another group that emerged from the community conversations, developed a long-term, aggressive plan for expanding the airport runway and facilities. This plan included negotiating a complicated financing plan with state and federal authorities. The plan required the community to raise large sums of money that would be leveraged by state and federal matching funds. Despite the benefits of the matching funds, the action team did not keep the community well informed of their ambitious plans. In addition, the Public Square steering committee failed to help the action team improve its communication with the larger community. One of the primary roles of the steering committee is to inform people about the happenings and successes of actions teams.

With rumors and information swirling regarding the details of the airport expansion plan, an angry and motivated citizen movement emerged. Using information that was incomplete and/or misleading, primarily because of the action team's failure to communicate, the citizen group garnered enough signatures on a petition to force the city council to either freeze airport development for ten years or hold a public referendum.

In turn, the city requested that the Public Square steering committee change a planned recreation community conversation to a community-wide conversation on airport development. The hope was that a facilitated public conversation would mediate the community conflict. That the city made this request was something of a breakthrough because it validated how much credibility the citizen-driven Public Square steering committee had gained with a city council that, heretofore, had been mostly hands-off with the Public Square process.

The steering committee complied with the city's request, postponed the planned recreation conversation, and agreed to facilitate the potentially volatile airport discussion. For the third time in about eighteen months, Public Square Communities, LLC, was called in to facilitate the public conversation. One hundred twenty community members attended and gathered around small tables with the diverse interest groups—action team, petitioners, city council, and steering committee—represented at each table. Both the action team and petitioners presented their cases. Then, each roundtable discussed what they heard and agreed upon a few questions that they felt needed to be answered. Table by table, they voiced their questions, and after each question, the facilitator asked if another table might have the answer to that question. After an hour, all questions had been answered, and the positions of both action team and petitioners had shifted from their opening statements. The evening closed with some strategic options to be researched and some complex questions clarified. Foremost, a general sense of goodwill had replaced a tension-filled room.

Reframing the Postponed Recreation Conversation

After the airport conversation, and before the postponed recreation conversation was rescheduled, an annual conference of all Public Square communities took place. At this conference, Public Square Communities, LLC, creates opportunities for every community involved in the process to share best practices and collaborate to overcome common challenges they are facing. On average about eighty-five people representing more than a dozen communities attend the conference. Gary and Jesse recruited a solid group of people to attend from their community. During the conference some members of their group went to another community's roundtable presentation about a very successful recreation program that coordinates and promotes over twenty volunteer-run recreation activities.

The group returned home excited that they had found another community that had managed to coordinate a wide range of free-standing recreation activities in a manner that alleviated scheduling conflicts and improved community participation. Instead of inviting a Public Square Communities facilitator to lead their recreation conversation, they asked three people to come from the county 150 miles away that had the successful program. The conversation took place, and the evening was a great success with a solid turnout of forty citizens. Here we have an example of the power of a real-time presentation from a peer community. In addition to making progress on recreation issues, there was an unexpected advantage of county-to-county relationships and cooperation.

Two years after Jesse and Gary had been chosen by their peers to be steering committee co-conveners, they have emerged as trustees of the common good. Gary and Jesse would be uncomfortable being credited with the success of these four community interventions. Yet they are exemplars of how to lead in civic spaces, in part because they enact a mediator role to transform win/lose or chaotic situations into cooperative ventures. Their way of convening the steering committee, which in turn convenes the larger community, has established a leadership style that is trusted and welcomed by the community.

KEY TERMS

collaboration

conflict

decision making

group boundaries and context

deliberating

leadership

listening

DISCUSSION QUESTIONS

1. How is the public square process, as described in this case, similar to and different from other types of group processes you have experienced?

2. Why do members of all four sectors of the "public square" need to be present in conversations like the ones depicted in this case? What problems/issues are appropriate for groups who consist of members from each sector of the public square to address?

3. What evidence of diversity do you see in these stakeholder groups? How can that diversity help or hinder decision making?

4. How would you describe Terry's leadership style? What are the strengths of this style for helping people understand the public square process?

5. Gary and Jesse used the public square process to mediate conflict in their community. How would you describe their approach to conflict management?

6. How would communities be affected if a process like the pubic square were embedded into every aspect of their public decision-making? What types of groups in your community would participate in this? How would they be organized? What would be some likely consequences and outcomes of their decisions?

ABOUT THE EDITORS AND CONTRIBUTING AUTHORS

Laura W. Black (Ph.D., University of Washington) is an assistant professor in the School of Communication Studies at Ohio University where she teaches graduate and undergraduate courses in small group communication. She studies public deliberation, dialogue, and conflict in small groups and is specifically interested in how personal storytelling functions in public forums. Her research of public meetings, juries, and online communities has appeared in *Communication Theory, Human Communication Research, Journal of Public Deliberation, Small Group Research, Political Communication*, and several edited books.

Courtney E. Cole (M.A., SUNY-Binghamton) is a doctoral candidate in the School of Communication Studies at Ohio University. Her research interests include narrative approaches to health, healing, and organizing processes, particularly in the contexts of conflict and suffering. Prior to pursuing her Ph.D., Cole worked in communications and research for several nonprofit organizations. Cole is a graduate teaching associate in the School of Communication Studies and has previously served as editorial assistant for *Health Communication*.

Abbey E. Wojno (M.A., Ohio University) is a doctoral student in the School of Communication Studies at Ohio University. Her current research interests are in the areas of organizational and health communication as well as women and gender studies. More specifically, she is interested in the work of nonprofit organizations and issues of voice, representation, the body, and agency. As a graduate teaching associate she teaches public speaking, techniques of group discussion, and interviewing.

Stephenson Beck (Ph.D., University of Kansas) is an assistant professor of communication at North Dakota State University. His research interests explore how group members strategically create messages, how group relationships are negotiated through interaction, and how group members create shared meaning through conversation.

Joseph A. Bonito (Ph.D., University of Illinois at Urbana-Champaign) is an associate professor in the Department of Communication at the University of Arizona. His primary research interests are small group interaction and influence, especially the interdependence of members' participation in relation to group outcomes. His research has appeared in *Human Communication Research, Communication Monographs, Communication Research, Small Group Research,* and *Communication Yearbook*.

Michelle Calka (M.A., Ball State University) is a doctoral student studying rhetoric and public culture in the School of Communication Studies at Ohio University. Her research interests focus on virtual communities and the performance of identity online, specifically through the representation and rhetorical functions of virtual bodies.

Martín Carcasson (Ph.D., Texas A&M University) is an associate professor in the Communication Studies department of Colorado State University and the founder and director of the CSU Center for Public Deliberation. His research focuses on the rhetoric of contemporary public affairs and the interdisciplinary theory and practice of deliberative democracy and collaborative governance. His research has been published in *Rhetoric & Public Affairs, International Journal of Conflict Resolution,* and *Quarterly Journal of Speech.*

Heather J. Carmack (Ph.D., Ohio University) is an assistant professor of communication in the Department of Communication at Missouri State University. Her research focuses on communication about medical mistakes and patient safety and the different ways in which health care is organized. She has published in journals such as *Health Communication, Journal of Medical Humanities, Qualitative Health Research,* and *Qualitative Research Reports in Communication.*

Levi Dexel (M.S., Ohio University) recently completed his degree in recreation and sport sciences at Ohio University. His master's thesis was a qualitative examination of group development within an adventure programming context. He is currently the coordinator of Outdoor Adventure Education at Duke University and teaches a variety of activity-based courses in outdoor recreation at Duke.

Logan Franken is an undergraduate honors student in the Department of Communication at the University of California, Santa Barbara. His research interests include the structuring of new technologies within organizations and the usability of computerized interfaces. He works as a freelance Web developer and designer. In his spare time he enjoys programming and bicycling.

Heidi K. Gardner (Ph.D., London Business School) is an assistant professor of organizational behavior at Harvard Business School. Her research examines the design of knowledge-intensive work, focusing in part on teams' use of expertise in professional service firms. She has published articles in *Academy of Management Journal* and *Journal of Organizational Behavior* and several chapters in edited volumes. Before academia, Gardner worked as a strategy consultant for McKinsey & Co. in London, Johannesburg, and New York and held a Fulbright fellowship in Germany. She earned a master's degree from the London School of Economics and a Ph.D. in organizational behavior from London Business School.

John Gastil (Ph.D., University of Wisconsin-Madison) is a professor of communication and political science at the University of Washington. His books include *The Jury and Democracy* (Oxford, 2010), *The Group in Society* (Sage, 2010), *Political Communication and Deliberation* (Sage, 2008), *By Popular Demand* (California, 2000), *Democracy in Small*

Groups (New Society Publishers, 1993), and the co-edited volume, *The Deliberative Democracy Handbook* (Jossey-Bass, 2005), and scholarly articles in various journals. The National Science Foundation has supported five large-scale research programs in which Gastil has served as a principal or co-investigator.

Annette N. Hamel (M.A., Ohio University) is a doctoral student in communication studies at Ohio University. Her primary area of study is relating and organizing, with a secondary emphasis on rhetoric and public culture. Her research interests center around communicating within and about difference, including in/out group communication and the rhetoric of race. She is particularly interested in the concept of diversity in the academy and how difference affects the student/teacher relationship. Among the courses she teaches are Public Speaking, Small Group Communication, Argumentation and Advocacy, and Interviewing.

Andrew P. Herman (Ph.D., Northwestern University, 2005) is an associate professor of communication at State University of New York at Geneseo where he teaches classes in personal and professional communication. His current research focuses on the role of relational communication in the formation of social capital and communication in the college classroom. Recent publications include co-written chapters in *Research on Social Problems and Public Policy* (Vol. 16) and *Communication Activism* (Vol. 2). Whenever possible, Herman involves students in his research and writing.

Paul Kang (M.A., University of California, Santa Barbara) is a doctoral candidate in the Department of Communication at the University of California, Santa Barbara. His research focuses on the role of communication in the development of teamwork.

Anne Gerbensky-Kerber (M.A., Minnesota State University, Mankato) is a doctoral student in the School of Communication Studies at Ohio University. Her research uses post-structural feminist and narrative theories to study issues at the intersections of health and organizational communication. These sensibilities direct her attention to issues of structure and agency that permeate organized initiatives and circulate within discourses about health. Specifically, she explores the contexts of school-based health initiatives and health-related policies.

Joann Keyton (Ph.D., The Ohio State University) is professor of communication at North Carolina State University. Her research interests are relational issues in teams, collaboration of interdisciplinary science teams, organizational culture, and sexual harassment. She is the editor of *Small Group Research*.

Stephen P. Konieczka (M.A., University of Colorado at Boulder) is a doctoral candidate in the Department of Communication, University of Colorado at Boulder. His research focuses on democratic discourse and discourses of democracy with particular attention to public policy development and discussion among small groups and gatherings. In addition to student governments, Stephen has written about deliberative, dialogic, and collaborative forms of public conversation, communication of interests and identity among groups developing public policy, and the tensions between order and disorder in democratic theory and practice.

Michael W. Kramer (Ph.D., Texas) is a professor and chair of the Department of Communication at the University of Oklahoma. His research primarily focuses on employee transitions, such as newcomer, transferee, and exit processes, along with other group processes. His recent work focuses on voluntary membership, particularly in community theater and choral groups. His books explore uncertainty management and socialization processes. This case study is based on his ethnographic study of the socialization of newcomers in a community choir.

Bruce Martin (Ph.D., University of Virginia) is an assistant professor in the Department of Recreation and Sport Pedagogy at Ohio University. His professional and scholarly interests are grounded primarily in outdoor leadership, a discipline that promotes safe, environmentally responsible use of the natural environment for recreational, educational, and therapeutic ends. He is interested in engaging in research and scholarship that helps to promote a tradition of evidence-based practice in the field of outdoor leadership, particularly in the area of outdoor leadership development.

Mridula Mascarenhas (M.A., University of Wisconsin-Milwaukee) is a doctoral student at the University of Wisconsin-Milwaukee and has taught at Ithaca College, NY as well as Saint Cloud State University, MN. Mridula is interested in the communication processes that occur in groups of all sizes and types, ranging from the small work group to larger communities. She is especially interested in studying communication from discursive and performative perspectives.

Erin McFee (M.B.A., Simmons School of Management) is a research associate in the Organizational Behavior Unit at Harvard Business School as well as in the Organizing for Health action-oriented research initiative. She has worked on research projects involving leadership teams and expertise use in team settings. Her independent research interests include the reconciliation and reintegration efforts in low-intensity conflict regions of Colombia, and she plans to pursue a Ph.D. in anthropology on the topic. McFee earned a master's degree from Simmons School of Management and her bachelor's in finance from Boston University.

Mary Meares (Ph.D., University of New Mexico) is an assistant professor of communication studies at the University of Alabama. Mary has taught intercultural, group, and organizational communication in the United States and Japan and was named the Faculty Mentor of the Year at Washington State University. Mary has also consulted for educational, corporate, and public service organizations in the areas of intercultural transitions, team building, and conflict. Her research focuses on intercultural groups, virtual teams, diversity in the workplace, and perceptions of voice. She has facilitated virtual group projects with students from China, Japan, Russia, and the United States.

Renee A. Meyers (Ph.D., University of Illinois) is a professor in the Communication Department at the University of Wisconsin-Milwaukee where she enjoys teaching group communication at the undergraduate and graduate levels. She is widely published. Her research interests include investigating group decision making and argument, communication in student classroom groups, and jury interaction. She also teaches courses on team decision making, conflict management, and effective meetings to a wide variety of organizational employees.

Marie D. Montondo (B.A., SUNY-Geneseo, 2010) completed her bachelor's in communication at State University of New York at Geneseo. A member of the Journalism and Media Studies track, Montondo's research focused on media portrayal of female politicians and international current events. Campus involvement includes participating in Lambda Pi Eta, the honorary student communication organization; writing for the college newspaper, *The Lamron*; and being a teaching assistant for small group dynamics. Her future plans are to pursue a graduate degree in media studies related to policy issues.

Leah M. Omilion (M.A., Wayne State University) is a doctoral candidate in the Department of Communication at Wayne State University and has previously spent several years working in the health care industry. She holds a variety of emergency communication and disaster preparedness certifications from the Federal Emergency Management Agency (FEMA). Her research focuses on organizational, small group, and crisis communication, with a particular interest in emergency response and clinical teams. She teaches courses in group, business, and organizational communication.

Margaret M. Quinlan (Ph.D., Ohio University) is an assistant professor of communication and a core faculty member of the Health Psychology Ph.D. Program at the University of North Carolina at Charlotte. Her scholarly work explores the organizing of health care resources and work opportunities for people with lived differences. She has published in *Health Communication, Text & Performance Quarterly, Journal of Research in Special Education Needs, Communication Teacher, Communication Education, Handbook of Health Communication*, and *Management Communication Quarterly*.

Justin Reedy (M.A. University of Washington) is a doctoral candidate in the Department of Communication at the University of Washington. His research focuses on political communication and group behavior. His research on political discussion and conversation, media use, and public opinion has appeared in *Political Psychology, University of Colorado Law Review, George Washington Law Review,* and *the Handbook of Internet Politics*.

Laura D. Russell (M.A. University of Dayton) is a doctoral candidate in the School of Communication Studies at Ohio University. Her current research explores the ways that narrative communication facilitates phenomenological understandings of recovery and well-being.

David R. Seibold (Ph.D., Michigan State University) is a professor of communication in the Division of Social Sciences (College of Letters and Science) and co-director of the

Graduate Program in Management Practice in the Technology Management Program (College of Engineering) at the University of California, Santa Barbara. His research interests include group communication and interpersonal influence, organizational innovation and change, management communication, and theory-practice issues.

Sarah Stawiski (Ph.D., Loyola University Chicago) is a postdoctoral research fellow at the Center for Creative Leadership (CCL) in Greensboro, NC. She has expertise in small group decision making, business ethics, and program evaluation. She has authored or coauthored a number of publications on these topics, to include the effects of ethical climate on group- and individual-level deception in negotiation and shared cognition and group learning. She has taught undergraduate courses in social psychology, research methods, and industrial/ organizational psychology. Dr. Stawiski holds a B.A. from the University of California, San Diego, and a Ph.D. in applied social psychology from Loyola University Chicago.

Timothy Steffensmeier (Ph.D., University of Texas, Austin) is an assistant professor of communication studies at Kansas State University, He teaches courses in Civic Leadership Communication, Communication & Democracy, and Rhetorical Theory. He also serves as a research associate with the Institute for Civic Discourse and Democracy. He has published a book, chapters, and essays focused on deliberative democracy, argumentation, and community visioning processes. These interests inform his scholarship concerning sustainable community development. Dr. Steffensmeier currently works with the Kansas Leadership Center and Public Square Communities, LLC on civic leadership and community building projects.

Leah M. Sprain (Ph.D., University of Washington) is an assistant professor of communication studies at Colorado State University where she also works with the Center for Public Deliberation. Her research and teaching draw on cultural communication perspectives to study local practices of democracy, including deliberation, environmental activism, and social movement rhetoric. She is a co-editor (with Danielle Endres and Tarla Rai Peterson) of *Social Movement to Address Climate Change*. Her work can also be found in *International Journal of Public Participation* and *Environmental Communication: A Journal of Nature and Culture*.

Tennley A. Vik (M.A., North Dakota State University) is a doctoral candidate in the School of Communication Studies at Ohio University. Her current research explores how sexual behavior is shaped by family communication.

Robert Whitbred (Ph.D., University of Illinois) is an assistant professor in the Communication Management Division in the School of Communication at Cleveland State University. His research interests include leadership processes in teams and organizations, understanding the influence of mission statements in organizations, and modeling emergent networks. Rob teaches undergraduate and graduate courses in team facilitation, small group theory, research methods, training, and organizational communication theory.

Terry Woodbury (M.Div., Princeton Theological Seminary) is president of Public Square Communities, LLC (2004–) and a frequent speaker on community development and civic leadership. He was president of the United Way of Wyandotte County (1997–2004) and a community consultant from 1990 to 1997. Terry founded/directed the Franklin Center, Inc. in Kansas City, KS (1979–1990). In 1992 he was the volunteer organizer of the All-America City Award for Wyandotte County. In 2002 he was named Wyandotte County Citizen of the Year (2002). Terry edited *Why Neighborhoods Work* (1995) and has published writings on community development, including a *National Civic Review* essay (Summer 2009) detailing the impact of the Public Square process on local government.